The Truth About Collaborating

The Truth About Collaborating

Why People Fail and How to Succeed

Dr. Gail Levitt

BEP | BUSINESS EXPERT PRESS

First published in 2020 by
Business Expert Press, LLC
222 East 46th Street, New York, NY 10017
www.businessexpertpress.com

ISBN-13: 978-1-94858-083-0 (paperback)
ISBN-13: 978-1-94858-084-7 (e-book)

Business Expert Press Human Resource Management and Organizational Behavior Collection

Collection ISSN: 1946-5637 (print)
Collection ISSN: 1946-5645 (electronic)

First edition: 2020

10 9 8 7 6 5 4 3 2 1

Printed in the United States of America.

Dedication

This book is dedicated to a few individuals in my inner circle who have inspired me over the years to develop a special interest in facilitating the collaboration process with teams.

From my mother, Marilyn Levitt, I acquired a natural curiosity about diverse people, and an appreciation for the special powers of intuition. These are two very essential traits for a successful collaboration.

My sister, Karen Levitt Morris, has been a positive role model to understand just how much constructive disagreement, as well as agreement, is crucial for an effective collaboration.

Watching my husband, George Geniev, make difficult choices about whether or not a collaboration is the best approach has given me valuable insights that have helped me in tough situations when I needed to do the same.

I would also like to acknowledge Dr. Kathryn Cook, my first mentor, who encouraged me to find strength in self-awareness, communication agility, and continuous improvement to help facilitate some of the most fulfilling collaborations ever.

I would like to thank J. Liz Saunders of The Virtual Alternative for her collaborative approach to editing and formatting this book.

I was inspired by the memory of my dear brother, Mark Elliot Levitt, who left this life all too soon, but who will always be remembered for his keen intellect and sensitivity.

Finally, I would like to acknowledge the positive influence of Becky, who made the tedious hours of writing in my office always pleasant due to her cheerful canine presence.

Abstract

This book takes a unique approach to collaboration by exploring the truth about collaboration failures and successes, based on exploring both the obstacles to and the solutions for collaborating successfully. It offers valuable strategies, best practices, techniques, tools, checklists, and templates for applying collaboration most efficiently, especially to achieve the following: build relationships and partnerships, solve business problems, make decisions, leverage conflicts, increase innovation, and stimulate transformation and change. Special features in this book include:

- Self-test: What are your collaboration strengths and weaknesses?
- Action planner: Checklist for planning an effective collaboration.
- Templates: Collaboration processes and techniques to implement.

Keywords

collaboration mindfulness; mindfulness; interpersonal communication; transformational leadership; conflict management strategies; conflict triggers; reframing messages; group collaboration processes; teamwork; facilitating group processes; communication agility; creative thinking techniques; transformative leadership; collaboration competencies; business vision; cultural adaptability; influencing without authority; collaboration teams; collaborative workplace

Contents

Introduction

Either attempt it not, or succeed.

—Ovid

Many organizations do a great job of promoting collaboration, but they fail to provide their people with the resources they need to succeed at it. This book is dedicated to those leaders and teams who are expected to collaborate in their daily work roles, and seek tools and techniques to help them do it well. Each chapter addresses a specific truth about collaboration in business: why a collaboration is likely to fail, and what to do instead to achieve collaboration success.

Chapter one addresses the number one reason why collaborations fail: unrealistic expectations and underdeveloped skill sets. It provides insights about how to set realistic expectations and identifies 10 core competencies for collaboration success:

1. Commitment
2. Connection
3. Curiosity
4. Convincing skills
5. Communication agility
6. Cultural adaptability
7. Courage
8. Creativity
9. Conflict resolution
10. Compliance

Chapter two explains how a lack of "collaboration mindfulness" can contribute to ineffective results. It also identifies how to achieve success based on a four-step process that can be remembered easily using the acronym "COIN": Committed, Open, Invested, and Nondefensive. It then offers 20 guidelines for achieving mental preparedness prior to and during collaborations that enable collaborators to gain the readiness and agility needed to overcome obstacles and achieve the best results.

Chapter three reveals that ineffective planning without a clear structure causes poor collaboration results. It introduces readers to the four components of a smooth collaboration process:

1. Discovery
2. Discussion
3. Disagreement
4. Agreement

Strategies and guidelines are provided for structuring and managing each component of the collaboration process most efficiently and effectively.

Chapter four addresses another reason why collaborations fail, namely the lack of a clear focus to which everyone agrees. This chapter emphasizes the importance of viewing both perspectives of the topic, as a problem or an opportunity, before committing to which one will be the most suitable choice to achieve the best outcomes. Practical guidelines for facilitating effective discussions for both problems and opportunities are featured.

Chapter five identifies inadequate questioning and poor influencing skills as key factors contributing to collaboration failures. It presents proven strategies for effective questioning, messaging, and persuading that enable collaborators to negotiate and influence decisions with agility and impact. This chapter reveals 12 types of influential questions to ask and concentrates on ways to motivate awareness, interest, commitment, and action using the "PARTNER" approach.

Chapter six explores how to navigate the emotional, physiological, and cognitive aspects of conflict in collaborations. It identifies poor conflict management as a contributing factor to failed collaborations and examines how to achieve successful collaborations by encouraging and managing disagreement strategically. The four conflict stages and strategies for managing each proactively are then discussed as follows:

1. Dormant
2. Emerging

3. Active
4. Aftermath

Chapter seven discusses narrow-minded thinking as a key reason why collaborators fail to achieve peak innovative solutions, and how to achieve success using more of a balanced, whole-brain thinking approach. This chapter offers guidelines for how to achieve maximum idea ownership and creativity by merging both left- and right-brain methods for the most creative options and solutions.

Finally, chapter eight reveals 10 common obstacles to the collaboration process as follows:

1. Unrealistic expectations about collaboration as a process.
2. Great difficulty scheduling meeting times and locations that are suitable for all parties.
3. Lack of accountability and commitment to follow through on promises.
4. Incompatible and dominant personalities.
5. Lack of integrated technology tools.
6. Team discomfort sharing knowledge and resources.
7. Lack of sponsorship from influential senior executive leaders.
8. Restrictive organizational bureaucracy limiting the ease of change initiatives.
9. Lack of diverse membership and representation.
10. Inadequate change leadership within the collaboration team.

Practical guidelines for overcoming each obstacle successfully are provided in detail.

CHAPTER 1

Collaborating Defined: What It Is and What It Is Not

Alone we can do so little; together we can do so much.
—Attributed to Helen Keller

Preview

This chapter discusses one key reason why people fail in collaborations: unrealistic expectations. It then explores how having a realistic understanding of what a collaboration is, and what it is *not*, results in the most successful outcomes. In this chapter, the misleading words, processes, and actions frequently mistaken for a collaboration are contrasted with what is actually required to enable a true collaboration to occur.

This chapter defines collaboration as a goal-oriented communication process that encourages both disagreement and agreement between two or more parties to identify and create a broader range of options, and determine the most beneficial solutions to a mutual problem or opportunity. The essential competencies to ensure a successful collaboration are identified and explained using the collaboration model, "The Decagon of Collaboration." Without these core capabilities, individuals are more likely to fail at collaboration than to succeed. These 10 capabilities include the following:

1. Commitment
2. Connection
3. Curiosity
4. Convincing skills
5. Communication agility
6. Cultural adaptability

   7. Courage
   8. Creativity
   9. Conflict resolution
  10. Compliance

Defining Collaboration

Collaboration is a word I hear almost daily on a professional and personal basis. For example, a client tells me that he would like to collaborate about an upcoming project. A senior executive informs me that her team needs to collaborate more to increase innovation. At a town hall meeting, a chief executive officer (CEO) emphasizes collaboration as a primary corporate priority that will help utilize resources better, increase teamwork, and improve overall organizational performance. At a project kickoff meeting, the sponsor refers to team collaboration as a crucial focus in a digital workplace. In a training workshop, a participant asks me how to build collaboration with someone who "does not want to collaborate." In a coaching session with a vice president of a major Canadian corporation, I am asked for efficiency tips about how to increase staff collaboration with limited time in a fast-paced, customer-focused environment.

Chances are that you or someone in your work or personal life has also emphasized the importance of collaboration. Perhaps a work colleague has said, "We need to collaborate" to indicate an interest in an honest dialogue about a mutual challenge or opportunity. Maybe a leader has informed you that collaboration is a core value for your organization, and expects you and others to demonstrate it as a model leader. Or consider a conversation with a business partner, client, or vendor who expresses an interest in developing your partnership through increased collaboration. A prospective employer might describe a workplace as a collaborative environment and ask you to explain how you can contribute to building a more collaborative culture, if you are hired to work there. At a monthly meeting, a book club member thanks the others for a collaborative discussion about a controversial book. In your personal life, your child might be involved in a collaborative learning project, or your physician might ask to work with you to collaborate on ways to promote healthy eating in your family. A lawyer might introduce collaboration as a method for managing a fair divorce settlement.

All of these examples illustrate that talking about one's intentions to collaborate is a positive motivation. Nonetheless, saying the word "collaboration" does not lead to a common understanding. The first step toward achieving a successful collaboration is to ensure that all parties involved agree on how to define what collaborating with each other means to them individually and as a group. Otherwise, there will be different interpretations about what occurred, and no way to guarantee that everyone will interpret that a collaboration actually happened.

One of my clients, a CEO of a large corporation, experienced this exact challenge firsthand. He spoke frequently and consistently about collaboration as a corporate value and priority for all staff, customers, business partners, and vendors, including at town hall meetings with staff. But he did not define the word "collaboration" specifically to any of his senior executives or their teams. In his view, this was not necessary.

When I was contracted by the company to help support the CEO's vision of more collaboration, I interacted over a two-year period with over 500 of his senior leaders and their staff for interviews, coaching, and training. I witnessed a high level of confusion, frustration, and disbelief regarding what he actually meant by using the word "collaboration." Some of the leaders and their staff assumed they were already collaborating, so they were offended by his asking them to do more of it, when they felt they were already delivering their best. Additionally, some individuals believed their approach to collaboration was better than that of others, and criticized some of their leaders and peers for not doing it well, which caused friction and conflict within the team. Still other members of the senior executive team were demotivated by the ambiguity of the CEO's request, expecting the CEO to communicate more clearly exactly what he meant by collaboration, so they knew how to put it into action.

After a series of debriefings and careful reviews of leader and staff feedback, the CEO finally agreed to communicate better with his senior executive team to cocreate a more specific corporate definition of collaboration that would then be conveyed consistently to all levels within the organization. The result was increased buy-in and commitment from the senior executive team. They were able to cocreate more tangible performance indicators to ensure that the CEO's vision was clear. Having a common understanding about what collaboration entailed in their organization also helped the leaders become more unified in achieving the vision that they felt more committed to supporting.

Agreeing about how to define collaboration is not the only way to understand it. Another way to comprehend what a true collaboration is, is to identify what it is *not*. Collaboration is *not* one-sided. Collaboration is *not* something one can accomplish solely with oneself; it requires the participation of one or more others to occur. Ultimately, collaboration is *not* possible if the others do not want to participate. Collaboration is *not* necessarily a safe or easy thing to do. This is because collaboration is *not* something that is inherently good or well received by others, as it involves some risks. Its motivations and outcomes can have negative as well as positive impacts that can be hard to predict or prepare for, depending on one's perspective. For example, collaborating on an innovative idea can be considered positive, whereas a war-time collaboration with the enemy based on power or coercion can be considered negative.

It is also crucial to understand that collaboration is *not* always the best way, or the right way, or the most approved way. Collaboration does *not* mean providing information or input that others have to agree with or respond to positively, so it is *not* the same as consensus. Collaboration is *not* based solely on agreement or compromise. Collaboration does *not* make collaborators more popular. Actually, collaborators can, in fact, be regarded more negatively if they offer opinions that are *not* commonly approved of by the rest of the team. Collaboration is *not* always effective, especially if it is perceived negatively, as inappropriate, as a waste of time, or is executed poorly. Collaboration is *not* a natural way for people to react, and it is *not* something that can be done easily without tremendous effort.

Additionally, collaboration is *not* a standardized, universal process. There is no one consistent, homogeneous approach that will work in every situation. It is *not* something that people do naturally and it is *not* easy to learn, either. Collaboration is *not* the same in each culture or organization because the individuals involved have diverse mindsets, beliefs, practices, and norms that define and demonstrate it differently. A collaboration does *not* have to be planned. It can occur proactively or spontaneously if all parties are like-minded in wanting to achieve the same goal or focus on a common interest. Collaboration does *not* look the same each time, so it is neither easy to identify in all situations nor obvious to explain.

So, when attempting to define what collaboration actually *is*, there are two commonly accepted definitions. The first one generally refers to working with others, typically using a formalized process, to produce or create something with a positive value to both parties, as in collaborating *with* another to achieve a common goal. In this context, the following words are often identified as related synonyms: groupings, teamwork, partnerships, associations, and alliance. The second definition typically identifies collaboration as a negative act of cooperation or treason, such as helping an enemy by providing information. These are some related words that one can associate within this context: conspiring, colluding, fraternizing, and betraying.

Although both definitions have very different motivations, the process is the same, namely providing information with some type of benefit in return. In the first example, collaborating for the purpose of producing something of value can result in improved status or image, shared pride, quality, better return on investment, happier customers, or enhanced teamwork. In contrast, as a negative act of collusion or conspiracy, collaboration with the enemy is more likely for the purpose of providing something of value to the other party for survival or self-preservation.

Regardless of whether it is for good or for bad, a collaboration cannot occur without another's active commitment and participation. It involves achieving results one could never accomplish on one's own by combining different skills, perspectives, information, and styles to achieve a common goal, outcome, result, or vision. This inevitably requires a special emotional climate and communication process for disagreement to ensure that diverse and differing views and perspectives are conveyed and truly heard in a safe group setting.

In essence, a collaboration is a contradiction in itself because to succeed, it needs to blend agreement on common principles, goals, and interests, with ample opportunity for disagreement. It is an ongoing process for both asserting ideas and building trusting relationships to express those ideas with all parties' interests in mind. Therefore, to succeed, collaborators need to attain a fine balance of assertiveness and trust that is complex and challenging to achieve.

Without a common goal, collaboration is most likely to fail due to the pressures that result from the two conflicting dynamics related to disagreement and agreement. To balance both equally, effective communication is necessary.

I recall an excellent example of a collaboration with a business partner that had the perfect balance of assertiveness and trust based on well-managed agreement and disagreement. For these reasons, that specific collaboration will always stand out in memory as one of the best I have ever experienced. Initially, we met to discuss an upcoming project and I learned that there was a team of about 12 people. I will name my key contact, a senior leader of the group, John. John had made a special effort to interview prospective business partners with the intent to hire the one with the most compatible values and complementary expertise. After asking and answering questions over a total of four meetings, two which we traveled to in person from two different cities, and two virtual meetings, John informed me of the good news that I was the vendor of choice for that project.

The first planning meeting by teleconference was a key turning point that consolidated our relationship to evolve into a true collaboration. The team members asked me to do a specific task for them a certain way, and assumed I would agree. However, I indicated that I preferred to do it another way. They were curious and open to hearing my approach, and they asked for clarification and an example. Motivated by their commitment to learn more about my course design process, I asked them many questions to understand their mindset and approaches. By the 10th weekly teleconference update, we were much more knowledgeable about each other and more aware of the thinking differences among us. Although it took much longer to get everyone's input, we established norms for disagreement to focus on better options and solutions without taking any criticisms or challenges personally.

Six months later, John and his team joined me for the training day. Each member sat at a table with other participants as a "champion" of the program. At breaks, we gave each other feedback about what was working and what needed improvement, and we brainstormed options together, sharing our commitment and accountability to ensure successful results. By the end of the session, I truly felt that this was our collective accomplishment. I would have done the training very differently if left on my own. It would have been faster and easier to work alone, but not as impactful. The participants rated the session the highest ever in the organization's history. And John and the team joined me to celebrate the incredible results of our collaboration.

That day was a reminder of Helen Keller's famous line, "Alone we can do so little; together we can do so much." Helen Keller (1880 to 1968) was a famous author, political activist, and lecturer. She could not see or hear, but based on the communication support of a team of people with complementary skills, she learned to speak and graduated from Radcliffe College of Harvard University in 1904 with a Bachelor of Arts degree, two very impressive accomplishments. Our team's relatively more modest achievement was to build a powerful, trusting relationship that enabled us to challenge each other for continuous improvement to achieve a goal that we accomplished with pride. Essentially, the quality of our communication was the key to our success.

Collaboration As a Communication Process

It is important for collaborators to remember not to take the process of communication for granted. The communication component of any collaboration begins with the complex process of encoding and decoding. This exchange includes conveying messages to others using words, tone, body language, silence, and intended meanings, and relying on them to decode the meaning accurately. When one party sends the information or input with the intent to convey specific information to the other party, there is no guarantee that mutual understanding will be achieved. When the receiver attempts to decode, or decipher what is transmitted, communication misunderstandings can easily occur due to differences in values, culture, language, experience, and interpretation. To achieve a common understanding, all collaborators need to invest considerable mental and emotional energy to clarify meanings for mutual understanding.

Demonstrating Collaboration Competencies

There are 10 essential competencies to ensure a successful collaboration for all concerned parties. I like to refer to these competencies as "The Decagon of Collaboration." They are as follows:

1. Commitment
2. Connection
3. Curiosity
4. Convincing skills
5. Communication agility
6. Cultural adaptability
7. Courage
8. Creativity
9. Conflict resolution
10. Compliance

1   *Commitment: To take accountability by investing time and energy to achieve a mutual end goal*

The first essential competency needed for a successful collaboration is commitment. This involves taking full accountability for the success of the collaboration, regardless of how much time and effort are needed to achieve the end goal. Being committed to the process of collaborating, as the best possible approach, also means believing in its power to achieve the desired outcomes. Investing mental and physical energy throughout the collaboration process entails having the emotional resiliency and the intellectual stamina to stay the course of the collaboration, without giving up. *Example: Recognizing that doing a project by oneself is faster, but deciding that collaboration is the best way to achieve innovation for that particular project.*

2   *Connection: To develop trust and community with the other parties*

Building strong connections with others is essential for a collaboration to succeed. Connecting with others to create a unified community of collaborators involves the skill to both give and receive direction, guidance, support, and criticism nondefensively in the spirit of cooperation and trust. To achieve this end, the collaborator needs a keen ability to observe others' emotional states nonjudgmentally and to be able to use that knowledge authentically with the best intention to establish an emotional climate of trust. To build trust, there needs to be a "you and me against the problem" mentality, not a "you are the problem" mindset. *Example: While collaborating on a new digital IT platform, you find out that one of the other team members in a different department is upset about a change. You decide to learn more about why that person objects, and concentrate on listening actively to what is said to understand, not to evaluate or judge. That other individual then asks you to talk about your attitudes in favor of the change and also listens without interrupting, while keeping an open mind. Although there is no immediate agreement about what to do next, both you and the other team member build more trust by knowing that you could express your views without argumentation, disapproval, or defensiveness. At the end of the conversation, you still do not agree, but you have each increased your understanding of the other's interests, and enhanced your trust as well.*

   3   *Curiosity: To explore new ideas and approaches outside one's own world view*

Curiosity is often underestimated as an essential competency for a successful collaboration. Wanting to know how others think, operate, work, and communicate is a positive motivator for any collaborator. It enables a true partnership that manages expertise and knowledge transfer with an openness to new ways of achieving the goal. Being curious creates the willingness to engage others to learn more about their concerns, motivations, suggestions, and goals with interest, patience, and tolerance. The result is more enjoyment of the collaboration process to explore the unknown, and the increased willingness to take risks to acquire new insights and skills based on trial and error, including broadening one's knowledge, based on making mistakes and reflecting on lessons learned, to put into action next time. *Example: During a collaboration, one of the team members, Jessie, objected to a process that Pat was explaining. Instead of responding defensively by justifying why the process needed to be followed and how it worked, Pat showed a natural curiosity by asking a series of questions to learn more about Jessie's concerns. During this process, Jessie's tone and manner became more relaxed, and he started to share more of his opinions. Throughout the discussion, Pat did a lot of paraphrasing to make sure that she understood Jessie's concerns and point of view, without pressuring him to agree to anything. At the end of the conversation, Pat informed Jessie that she appreciated the time he took to explain his concerns. As a result of her curiosity, Pat was able to learn more about Jessie's thinking process and earn his trust for future brainstorming discussions throughout the collaboration.*

4   *Convincing skills: To influence buy-in and manage disagreement proactively*

The ability to influence others, both with and without authority, is one of the most important competencies needed to achieve success in a collaboration. Fluent convincing skills require a combination of talents: an understanding of the difference between informing and influencing, the verbal and written agility to reframe messages with the intent to persuade, the capacity to think quickly on one's feet, and an understanding of negotiation strategies and tactics to apply in different situations, as the need arises. *Example: During an intense debate involving a lot of disagreement, you notice that the comments are adversarial and not constructive. So you convince the collaboration team members to refocus on the purpose of their debate. You get their agreement to a common goal, namely improving customer service quality and delivery times. Once you achieve their buy-in and commitment, you are able to encourage and manage their disagreement by establishing and enforcing "ground rules", and reminding the group that improving customer service quality and delivery times is the end goal.*

5   *Communication agility: To convey constructive messages fluently and skillfully*

In any collaboration, responding spontaneously to unexpected questions with competence and credibility requires considerable communication agility. An agile communicator has the skill and self-confidence to think on his or her feet quickly and demonstrate the flexibility to adapt the message to engage the other collaboration parties. Being able to handle ambiguous information and questions with confidence and reframe one's response with a clear focus on the collaboration goals are key components of communication agility. *Example: During a collaborative negotiation session, a business partner assumed that the other party had agreed to implement a new process. But the other party had not agreed yet to the process and expressed some serious concerns in an aggressive way that was emotionally charged. The business partner demonstrated communication agility by rephrasing the question to ensure her complete understanding of the concern. She then reframed the focus to the common goal and explained nondefensively how the new process would achieve the expected outcomes. This communication agility to de-escalate the conversation and address challenges more constructively enabled the business partner to build trust and understanding with the other party throughout the remainder of the collaboration.*

6   *Cultural adaptability: To observe and adjust well to diverse values, beliefs, and norms*

The ability to observe, adjust, and adapt to different cultural norms, beliefs, and practices is necessary for any collaboration to succeed. Cultural adaptability entails the awareness and sensitivity to recognize important cultural differences that need to be noticed and addressed to build rapport and enable effective communication. Collaborators with cultural adaptability are thoughtful and deliberate about how they communicate, taking into consideration others' different beliefs and attitudes about time, technology, authority, conflict, teamwork, decision making, negotiation, and collaboration meeting norms.

Since collaborations require a significant investment of time, effective time management is essential. Understanding how different cultures perceive and utilize time can be a crucial advantage for any collaborator interested in achieving high engagement as well as maximum productivity for successful outcomes. There are two contrasting time values. Those cultures preferring monochronic time, or m-time, see time as linear, sequential, structured, and not to be wasted. They integrate these values into collaborations by insisting on having detailed agendas, strict timelines, and documented follow-up for planned actions. Cultures considered to be monochronic include Germany and England.

Cultures that prefer polychronic time, or p-time, perceive time as more spontaneous and free flowing, with a "we will get there when we get there" attitude. Collaborators with a polychronic focus on time enjoy a more open-ended approach to meetings without the need for much written documentation or structure. They prefer to leave lots of unscheduled time for unforeseen opportunities and enjoy the freedom of responding in the moment and not being obligated to follow a strict agenda. One can identify monochronic and polychronic time values through observation, asking questions about preferences, and trial and error. Cultures that are considered polychronic include Brazil and France. If one is not sure about the team's attitudes toward time, it is best to organize the collaboration meetings to include a blend of polychronic and monochronic elements. *Example: During a collaboration session, one individual from a monochronic culture insisted on an agenda with the specific start and end times for each topic. However, another participant from a polychronic culture objected, saying that an agenda was not necessary, and that it would be better to just "go with the flow." The collaboration facilitator was very familiar with m-time cultures that see time as linear, and with p-time cultures that prefer a less structured approach. So the facilitator recommended a compromise to appeal to both parties by simplifying the agenda to be less detailed and more open-ended. Both parties agreed, knowing that making small adjustments would demonstrate their commitment to building a partnership that was strengthened by different cultural expectations of what makes a collaboration meeting most productive.*

7   *Courage: To take risks beyond one's comfort zone to try new approaches*

Having the courage to take risks, despite some discomfort, can lead to more successful outcomes in collaborations. The courage to trust someone else's expertise or try a new approach offers the potential for more innovative options and solutions. The courage to voice unpopular or different viewpoints and try new approaches requires the mindset of an explorer and adventurer. There is always the risk of uncertainty regarding whether or not the desired end results will be achieved. Nonetheless, the courage to strive for something new and different and trust in one's intuition is an essential part of the collaboration journey. *Example: Mary's collaboration team member, James, has recommended a new process, the XYZ methodology, but Mary has never tried it before. Mary is open to trying it on a pilot basis, but Mary's boss is suspicious about using it at all because there is no statistical data available to support its potential success or failure. However, James has used this process before, in a former job in another organization, and claims that it will be ideal for the project Mary is working on. After careful review of the facts with her collaboration team colleague, Mary agrees to take a risk and recommend to her boss that a test pilot be implemented to try the new process and evaluate its effectiveness. If the process fails, Mary could receive negative feedback from her boss, or even a demotion. If Mary succeeds, the organization will benefit with more efficiency and cost savings, and she could gain more credibility with her boss and other leaders, even eligibility for a promotion. Mary's courage leads her to take the risk with the support of her collaboration team, including her boss. Six months later, Mary provides her boss with a summary of the cost savings and high customer praise for the new process. Shortly after, Mary's boss approves a proposal from the collaboration team for a new partnership to implement the XYZ process for the organization for all locations globally.*

8   *Creativity: To apply both divergent and convergent brainpower*

Achieving peak creativity for innovative solutions is what drives the collaboration process. Exploring and inventing new options and approaches, that others might never have considered alone, is one of the most exciting ways a collaboration team can achieve success. The biggest obstacle to achieving peak creativity in a collaboration occurs when team members rely too much on proven approaches or delude themselves into thinking that they have generated creative options, when those ideas are not very creative at all. Limiting one's thinking style to either a logical, left-brain approach or a more intuitive, right-brain focus can restrict a collaboration team's potential to achieve peak creativity. The best approach is to combine both left- and right-brain methods when attempting to generate the most innovative ideas. This requires blending both right-brain, divergent thinking and more left-brain, convergent thinking approaches. Whereas convergent thinking involves wanting to know the correct answers to analyze and solve problems logically and systematically based on data and logic, divergent thinking is the opposite. Divergent thinking is a more intuitive approach to generate as many options as possible, even if they are not practical or correct. It involves thinking more conceptually and less practically.

In contrast, convergent thinking involves narrowing down the options as quickly as possible to avoid ambiguity, often achieved by devising operational procedures and a tactical action plan. The divergent approach to problem solving, also known as lateral thinking, involves a more free flowing and less linear process that poses more questions than answers to address alternative options based on supposition and the imagination. *Example: During a team meeting to collaborate on a new process for tracking project results, a convergent thinker recommended a specific product based on quantitative data that supports it for being the most accurate, affordable, and easy to implement quickly. In contrast, a divergent thinker on the team provided 20 different ideas for ways to track results, including unique options based on interviewing people in different industries who created their own products using visual, state-of-the-art technology adapted from the graphics and movie industries. The final solution combined both approaches, resulting in the best use of the collaboration team's brainpower, ultimately achieving the most creative results possible.*

9   *Conflict Resolution: To manage conflicts confidently using proven strategies and tactics*

Since disagreement is a natural part of a collaboration, having proficient conflict resolution skills is critical for success. Being self-aware of one's own conflict reactions and being able to address others' conflict responses with calm and confidence require special training and practice. The self-awareness to recognize and manage conflict "triggers" proactively involves self-reflection and discipline. Knowing what strategies to apply to manage disagreements without unnecessary escalation requires an understanding of conflict styles and the knowledge of appropriate conflict management strategies to use with deliberation and flexibility. Constructive feedback from others based on how to handle conflict situations better can also help develop resiliency and adaptability. *Example: When acting as the lead negotiator during a contract negotiation with multiple parties, Fred was able to reduce people's frustration and reframe their discussion to build on their different opinions, resulting in contractual changes that all parties agreed were beneficial. Fred's self-awareness of his own conflict responses enabled him to avoid taking the others' comments too personally. Fred's familiarity with proven conflict strategies enabled him to plan and implement a variety of techniques that helped him gain control of the discussion without being perceived as too controlling.*

10   *Compliance: To construct and enforce consistent group processes and protocols to ensure a successful collaboration*

Team collaborations involve much more than idea generation and trust building. They also require compliance to policies, legislation, decision-making standards, and group processes to get things done thoroughly and efficiently. Therefore, it is essential for all collaboration parties to identify legal and administrative requirements and adhere to them consistently to ensure that ethical and legal standards are maintained to achieve quality results that are suitable for all. Additionally, it is important to create and enforce group communication processes to ensure that the team is able to function most efficiently and effectively to build productive partnerships and achieve the desired goals. Group operating norms include processes regarding discussing, debating, disagreeing, updating, deciding, and making changes. Although a collaboration does not need to be formal, it does typically require consistent norms and protocols that are followed routinely by everyone so that there is maximum engagement and participation. *Example: To enable effective collaboration, the project leader engaged the group in agreeing to "ground rules" for behavioral norms at both virtual and in-person meetings. This included agreeing on how the group would interact during meetings to build trust, manage disagreement, make decisions, and agree to roles and responsibilities. These "ground rules" were communicated to all team members at the beginning of all meetings. Periodically, the team reviewed these norms and demonstrated ownership by contributing to and voting for "ground rule" modifications and additions when necessary.*

Summary

Defining collaboration is not an easy task because it is an often-used and misunderstood word and process. Misconceptions of collaboration include mistaking it as a general partnership, having universal characteristics, involving standard norms for behavior, and generally serving as the primary means for agreement. Collaboration is defined in this chapter as a goal-oriented process that encourages both disagreement and agreement between two or more parties to achieve a broader range of options and solutions for a mutual problem or opportunity.

The purpose of a collaboration can be for good or for bad. Collaboration can lead to results that one could never accomplish on one's own. Any collaboration requires the active commitment of at least two individuals for it to take place. It encourages disagreement as well as agreement to blend different skills, perspectives, information, and styles to achieve a common goal, outcome, result, or vision.

The 10 essential competencies for a successful collaboration, known as "The Decagon of Collaboration," are as follows:

1. Commitment: To invest time and energy on an end goal.
2. Connection: To develop trust and community with the other parties.
3. Curiosity: To explore new ideas and approaches beyond one's world view.
4. Convincing skills: To influence buy-in and manage disagreement proactively.
5. Communication agility: To convey constructive messages fluently and skillfully.
6. Cultural adaptability: To observe and adjust well to diverse values, beliefs, and norms.
7. Courage: To take risks beyond one's comfort zone to try new approaches.
8. Creativity: To apply both convergent and divergent brainpower.
9. Conflict resolution: To manage conflict confidently using proven strategies and tactics to both encourage and manage disagreement.
10. Compliance: To construct and enforce consistent group communication processes and protocols to make sure discussions involve disagreement as well as agreement to generate the best options and solutions.

CHAPTER 2

Practicing "Collaboration Mindfulness"

Many ideas grow better when transplanted into another mind than in the one where they sprang up.

—Oliver Wendell Holmes

Preview

This chapter identifies "collaboration mindfulness" as the first step to achieving successful outcomes. It defines this mental attitude as a combination of four key traits that are summarized in the acronym "COIN": committed, open, invested, and nondefensive. In this chapter, 20 guidelines relating to "COIN" are explained that can help achieve the mental preparedness that collaborators need to manage their expectations, energy, attitude, and time proactively for optimal results.

Acquiring "Collaboration Mindfulness"

An important truth about collaborating successfully is that it has to be a state of mind first, before any actions can lead to achieving meaningful results. A positive mental perspective is what enables collaborators to withstand and adapt to the ups and downs of the complex process of collaborating. Being adequately prepared mentally and emotionally gives a collaborator the stamina, confidence, and resiliency to stay focused on the end goal. This "collaboration mindfulness" is a powerful secret of success for any collaborator, and when it is absent, it can contribute to the failure of a collaboration.

Practicing "collaboration mindfulness" leads to a sense of calm, so one can concentrate on what is most important in a collaboration: inquiry and exploration. According to Tracy Page, PMP, Adjunct Professor, University of British Columbia, Sauder School of Business, "collaborating successfully means quieting our own minds and our need to move to the next deliverable as quickly as possible. It requires ensuring there is enough time to express ideas, ask lots of questions, listen genuinely for answers; and be willing to do this more than once."[1]

The four essential mental traits required for "collaboration mindfulness" can be summarized using the acronym "COIN":

1. *Committed*—Convinced that collaboration is the best process for achieving the desired results.
2. *Open*—Willing to consider alternative ideas, options, methods, and solutions that one would not typically think of, consider, or agree to on one's own.
3. *Invested*—Willing to dedicate the necessary time and effort to develop a trusting and united partnership with the other collaborators.
4. *Nondefensive*—Able to converse with and challenge other collaborators without the mental and emotional distractions of one's own defensive or territorial thinking.

Each one of these traits is a special mental attribute that represents a deliberate and meaningful way to be prepared for both the expected and unpredictable aspects of the collaboration process (Table 2.1).

The first trait is mental commitment, a best-kept secret for collaboration effectiveness. The deliberate mental act of choosing to participate in a collaboration demonstrates a collaborator's accountability from the very beginning. This accountability involves the collaborator's mental fortitude to follow-through on commitments and actions, regardless of any obstacles and difficulties encountered along the way. The second trait, being open to others' ideas and suggestions, requires the mental and emotional readiness to expand one's thinking beyond the limits of one's own ideas, experiences, and expertise. Listening actively to what others say, even if one does not agree, can be tough on one's ego. However, being

---

[1] Page, Tracy, PMP, Adjunct Professor, University of British Columbia, Sauder School of Business. March 18, 2019. E-mail message to author.

Table 2.1 Defining "collaboration mindfulness"

C	ommitted	To invest time and energy in the collaboration process
O	pen	To acknowledge alternative ideas, options, methods, and solutions one would not ordinarily consider on one's own.
I	nvested	Willing to dedicate the effort to develop trusting and united partnerships
N	ondefensive	Able to think and communicate beyond one's own territorial thinking by managing mental and emotional distractions.

open to consider the best ideas, regardless of who gets credit for them, can help increase the possibility that the end result of the collaboration will be especially unique, innovative, and effective.

The third trait of "collaboration mindfulness" is being willing to invest the necessary time and energy to develop meaningful partnerships by valuing people as the highest priority. This attitude requires the mental determination and emotional strength to invest time and effort to build a strong, trusting bond with others. Prioritizing relationships above work schedules and deadlines is not an easy task in today's workplace, so patience and a commitment to the collaboration team are essential for building strong relationships with all involved parties. According to Anson Tung, Director, Open Enrolment, Sauder School of Business, The University of British Columbia, "collaboration mindfulness" consists of three key ingredients, namely team collaboration, compassion, and trust: "Collaboration mindfulness simply means to be compassionate and foster an emotional connection to all internal and external team members to enable trust and collaboration to take place authentically. I think this is the basis for a successful collaboration: understanding each person's needs, and developing trust."[2]

The fourth trait of "COIN" is being nondefensive in one's thinking. A nondefensive reaction in a collaboration can empower others to voice their views more freely and even give negative feedback with confidence.

---

[2] Tung, Anson, Director, Open Enrolment. *Director, Open Enrolment, UBC Sauder School of Business.* The University of British Columbia. April 5, 2019. E-mail message to author.

The ability to be receptive to the input of others without the need to overjustify or protect one's own position requires the self-awareness to recognize one's own defensiveness, and the self-discipline to restrain and control unnecessary territorial thinking.

Twenty Guidelines for Mental Preparedness

Implementing the four traits of "collaboration mindfulness" into actions is challenging, but it is achievable with the right attitudes and behaviors. The following 20 guidelines listed below can help collaborators develop and demonstrate the appropriate mental readiness and resiliency necessary to achieve success ultimately:

1. *Take all the time you need*

Successful collaborations require sufficient time to do them right, so they tend to proceed slowly. Taking all the time you need requires not seeking agreement too early in the collaboration process, and recognizing that the journey cannot be rushed if one wants to achieve optimal results. For a results-oriented individual, valuing quick decisions to get things done, and being deliberate about taking the time necessary to hear everyone's opinions, are the greatest challenges. Skilled collaborators know that a deadline-driven conversation emphasizing quick agreement to move forward to take action and schedule deadlines can erode trust if used too early and too often. They understand the importance of taking all the time necessary to discuss, disagree, explore, and create the best possible strategies, options, and solutions first. They also avoid getting distracted too soon by more operational details such as deadlines, budgets, and resources that they can address later in the process, once trust has been established.

2. *Stay focused on the collaboration goal*

The goal of a collaboration is the glue that connects all parties. It is the common vision or expected outcome that drives all discussions and connects people. Keeping the goal in mind at all times can help the parties ensure that discussions are productive and people are unified with a common focus throughout the entire process. An example of a collaboration goal is increasing customer satisfaction for a certain product or service. The best way to keep the collaboration goal top of mind is to get agreement from all parties involved, and refer to it consistently in meetings, documentation, and correspondence.

3. *Consider all possibilities*

Narrow-minded thinking that avoids exploring all possibilities can result in less than ideal options and solutions for a collaboration. An option or an idea that is rejected because of a perceived limitation, such as costs or resources, can seriously jeopardize the potential of the collaboration to inspire innovation and change.

4. *Accept that your way of thinking and doing things is not the only way, the best way, or the right way.*

During collaborations, it can be very difficult at times to listen to others' opinions without insisting that one's own ideas are best. However, experienced collaborators acknowledge that promoting one's own views as superior can cause the erosion of trust by appearing to be too self-righteous or close-minded to others' views. Acknowledging to oneself and others that one's own way of thinking and acting is just one of many different approaches is crucial for the best conversations and information exchanges in a collaboration.

5. *Focus on "we" instead of "me" thinking and shared ownership of ideas generated*

Cocreating ideas and solutions is the key purpose of a collaboration. With "we" thinking, the end results will be greater than what any one individual can accomplish on his or her own. Increased buy-in and commitment also results from shared ownership of what is discussed, explored, created, and decided. This means that options and solutions need to be suitable to all parties, and not just one or two individuals who are most persuasive, have more political power, or control the greatest amount of money in the budget.

6. *Accept the ambiguity of not knowing all the answers*

Ambiguity is a positive asset for any collaboration. Not having a concrete approach or answer can actually stimulate open dialogue to examine new ideas based on proposing and examining different ways to approach a problem or opportunity. Some key words that can help encourage a tolerance for ambiguity in a discussion about possibilities include: "what about….?," "what if…?," and "why not?"

7. *Always ask questions to enhance your understanding of others' perspectives*

Collaborating is an exploratory process that is more about asking the right questions than knowing the correct answers. Questioning others about their interests, ideas, and concerns encourages discussion about new approaches and solutions that one would not ordinarily conceive of on one's own. It also facilitates an active dialogue without the pressure of having to reach an agreement. Broadening one's understanding based on others' views can only benefit the entire collaboration team to help them assess a problem or opportunity with more depth and breadth of thinking.

8. *Assume that all collaboration partners have equal status and titles*

Although it is important to be knowledgeable about the actual titles and status of all collaboration parties to understand their unique perspectives and possible motivations, perceiving them as being equal helps to unite the group as a consolidated "us" and "we."

The intent of suspending differences in title, status, and roles is to eliminate barriers between all parties. It also creates a commonality that establishes the clear expectation that everyone's importance, knowledge, experience, and input is of equal quality and value. Removing barriers to equality helps establish an emotional climate designed to eliminate hierarchy, power, and territorial behaviors to enable more meaningful discussion and information sharing based on considering each individual's contribution as having equal importance.

9. *Focus on making changes for the future, instead of revisiting the past*

The purpose of a collaboration is to plan changes for the future. The risks of focusing too much on the past can cause teams to focus less on what will happen next and become distracted by details, justifications, and politics of what has already taken place. Dwelling too much on the past can also limit available time to explore options and solutions for the present and future.

10. *Take the time to relax mentally and physically*

The collaboration process requires both mental and physical stamina to manage team dynamics to integrate diverse ideas to determine the best solutions. Taking the necessary time to relax, mentally and physically, reduces one's stress and increases one's energy, focus, and motivation to stay the course to the end of the collaboration.

11. *Trust yourself first, so you can find it easier to trust others*

Building trust with other collaboration parties is difficult to achieve without trusting in oneself first. Self-acceptance and belief in the power of one's inner voice are all related to trusting oneself, therefore making it easier to extend that trust to others as well.

12. *Remember that there is no "I" in empathy, but there is a "Y" in "You"*

It is difficult to have empathy for someone else when too preoccupied with one's own individual experiences, problems, or needs. It is much easier to demonstrate empathy when one removes one's own ego and responses from one's mind and concentrates on imagining oneself in the other party's place. Empathy does not mean agreement. Empathy requires understanding another's views and experiences and not expecting them to necessarily be the same as yours, without needing to agree or disagree.

13. *Accept disagreement nondefensively so you can truly learn from and listen to others*

When challenged by someone who disagrees and believes he or she is right, there is a natural tendency to start thinking about a rebuttal, complete with reasons justifying how and why the other individual is wrong. However, this type of defensive thinking restricts one's capacity to concentrate on what the other is saying. Instead, it is better to encourage disagreement without a defensive response by avoiding interruptions, and using the time as an opportunity to listen and learn. Self-righteous thinking that one's approach is the best or the most expedient also defeats the purpose of a collaboration to integrate diverse ways of thinking and doing for the benefit of all. It is vital to recognize that your way of thinking and doing things is not necessarily the only way, the right way, or the best way. Experienced collaborators keep an open mind, knowing that just because they feel strongly about an option or solution, they still need the buy-in and commitment from the team to take accountability for all decision making.

14. *Listen for understanding, not agreement*

Listening without judgment is a difficult process, especially when one does not agree with what is being said. In collaborations, there is a high probability that people might say things that you and some others do not agree with. Knowing that understanding is more important than agreement makes it easier to listen more actively in order to comprehend, without the immediate need to evaluate or approve of what is being said.

15. *Have the self-confidence to convey your ideas assertively*

Conveying an assertive message requires the self-confidence to believe that what one has to say has value and deserves to be heard and acknowledged. Assertive collaborators believe they have the right to express and defend their views confidently and respectfully, without the need to impose those ideas on others forcefully. They also use the accountable pronoun, "I," to indicate their own individual concerns and feelings, rather than generalizing about others without their consent and using the pronoun "we" when it actually only represents "I."

16. *Encourage others to convey their ideas assertively*

In a collaboration, it is vital for all parties to express their views assertively without any fear of reprisals. A lack of assertiveness can shut down a collaborative discussion very quickly, causing a lack of diverse ideas. Wanting to include and support others through active engagement in a collaborative discussion is a strong motivator for encouraging them to participate actively. Believing that others have something worthwhile to say and recognizing the importance of different opinions are good reasons for encouraging others to assert themselves honestly, and with confidence.

17. *Communicate deliberately with honesty and tact*

Honest communications are vital for collaborative partnerships to develop trust and authenticity. Although honesty is essential in any collaborative partnership, it is easier for other parties to listen and understand if the message is also delivered diplomatically. Being authentic and deliberate, and using words that are tactful, help engage others to listen and reduce the risk that they will interpret the comments too personally.

18. *Follow a systematic communication process*

Open communications in collaborations do not just happen randomly without effective planning. There has to be some type of deliberate structure to manage the communication process to ensure effective discussion, disagreement, and decision making. There are a variety of ways to manage the flow, tone, content, participation levels, and time efficiency of collaborator interactions, including: "ground rules" for acceptable norms of behavior, a meeting agenda, a seasoned facilitator, and an agreed-upon decision-making processes.

19. *Remain curious about others' perspectives*

Curiosity about how others perceive and do things enables collaborators to sustain a high level of interest and engagement throughout the process. Wanting to know as much as possible about the other parties' attitudes, beliefs, practices, and suggestions serves as a natural motivator; this will enable curious individuals to value information sharing as a good use of their time. This curiosity enables them to be very effective in building strong partnerships with the other parties in the most natural way that demonstrates genuine interest and trust.

20. *Focus on growing instead of winning*

Collaboration should not be a game about winners and losers. It is a growth process that enables the collaborator to learn continuously through trial and error. In the true spirit of a successful collaboration, focusing on self-growth through continuous improvement is much better than winning anything. Learning more about new ways to think, respond, and take action is fundamental to a "collaboration mindset."

Summary

The first step toward a successful collaboration is to develop mental agility based on a realistic and adaptive attitude about what to expect, and the patience to slow down and reflect. This "collaboration mindfulness" serves as an effective foundation for mental and physical resiliency to endure the challenges and changes involved in the collaboration process. It also provides an essential level of mental preparedness about what to expect, realistically, to help collaborators avoid giving in or giving up, or even failing due to impatience, disappointment, or disillusionment.

The four key traits of "collaboration mindfulness" can be summarized using the acronym, "COIN," as follows:

1. *Committed*—Convinced that collaboration is the best process for achieving the desired results.
2. *Open*—Willing to consider ideas and approaches that one would not typically think about or consider if left on one's own.

3. *Invested*—Willing to dedicate the necessary time and effort to develop a trusting and united partnership with the other collaborators.

4. *Nondefensive*—Able to converse and argue with other collaborators without the mental interference of defensive or territorial thinking.

There are 20 guidelines for applying "collaboration mindfulness" to achieve success in a collaboration.

1. Take all the time you need.
2. Stay focused on the collaboration goal.
3. Consider all possibilities.
4. Accept that your way of thinking and doing things is not the only way, the best way, or the right way.
5. Focus on "we" versus "me" thinking with shared ownership of ideas generated.
6. Accept the ambiguity of not knowing all the answers.
7. Always ask questions to enhance your understanding of others' perspectives.
8. Assume that all collaboration partners have equal status and titles.
9. Focus on making changes for the future, instead of revisiting the past.
10. Take the time to relax mentally and physically.
11. Trust yourself first, so you can find it easier to trust others.
12. Remember there is no "I" in "empathy," but there is a "Y" in "You."
13. Accept disagreement nondefensively so you can truly listen and learn from others.
14. Listen for understanding, not agreement.
15. Have the self-confidence to convey your ideas assertively.
16. Encourage others to convey their ideas assertively.
17. Communicate deliberately with honesty and tact.
18. Follow a systematic communication process.
19. Remain curious about others' perspectives.
20. Focus on growing instead of winning.

CHAPTER 3

Collaborating As a Process

Coming together is a beginning, staying together is progress, and working together is success.

—Henry Ford

Preview

This chapter explores collaborating as a systematic process. It recommends how to plan, guide, and direct each phase of a collaboration proactively. In this chapter the four phases of a collaboration are identified as follows:

1. Discovery
2. Discussion
3. Disagreement
4. Agreement

This chapter addresses the unique challenges of each phase and reviews techniques for how to achieve optimal results for success.

Strategies are offered for how to recognize and manage each phase most efficiently and effectively.

Preparing for Success

Collaborating is a very demanding undertaking requiring extensive preparation, commitment, focus, and flexibility to build the partnerships required for success. However, sometimes there are special moments in a collaboration when discussion happens smoothly and naturally, without much planning or preparation. In those unexpected situations, team members connect and exchange ideas about a mutual problem or opportunity freely and easily. All parties appear to work together well to discuss a common goal effortlessly. They feel exhilarated and energized by the experience of cocreating options and solutions. When the discussions end and the goal is achieved, they all agree that they have accomplished something meaningful together, with everyone contributing equally.

There can be any number of reasons why in some collaborations, the parties relate to each other so well. This can include common backgrounds or experiences, personality compatibility, or just plain luck. Since these spontaneous connections are not the norm, they should be appreciated when they do occur. I recall working on a government project once when there was a strong team synergy from the very beginning that enabled effective collaboration immediately. None of us knew each other before, but we were able to agree on ideas quickly and support each other in a short time with strict deadlines and limited resources. Each person took accountability to commit to promises and complete tasks on time. We felt as if we were on a dream collaboration team and were disappointed when the project ended and we were assigned to work on different teams. I then experienced a series of collaborations involving partnerships that eventually gained trust and candor, but would never compare to the instant and lasting connections I experienced with my previous team colleagues on that government project.

The truth is that it is risky to assume that synergistic and productive collaboration discussions happen automatically. It takes a lot of time, effort, and skill for a collaboration to be both productive and successful. Collaborating is a complex communication process that needs to be planned, organized, structured, monitored, and evaluated systematically to sustain it on an ongoing basis. Understanding how that process works and being able to identify and manage each phase with successful collaboration management can help ensure strengthened partnerships and outstanding outcomes without relying on luck.

Understanding the Collaboration Process

There are four phases that typically characterize a collaboration:

- *Discovery:* Explore purpose, people, and perceptions.
- *Discussion:* Exchange information, ideas, and suggestions.

- *Disagreement:* Address objections and differences proactively.
- *Agreement:* Finalize decisions, contracts, responsibilities, and actions.

Each phase of a collaboration can occur in a sequence, or in a nonlinear pattern. When one or more of these phases is omitted or underdeveloped, the success of the collaboration could be at risk (Figure 3.1).

The *Discovery* phase is typically the beginning of a collaboration. The key purpose of the Discovery phase is to explore different perceptions among the parties involved to learn more about overall similarities and differences in assumptions, goals, perspectives, skills, and expectations. This phase requires sufficient time to build strong relationships with the other parties, encourage the collection and exchange of information, and facilitate an open emotional climate to foster the sharing of different

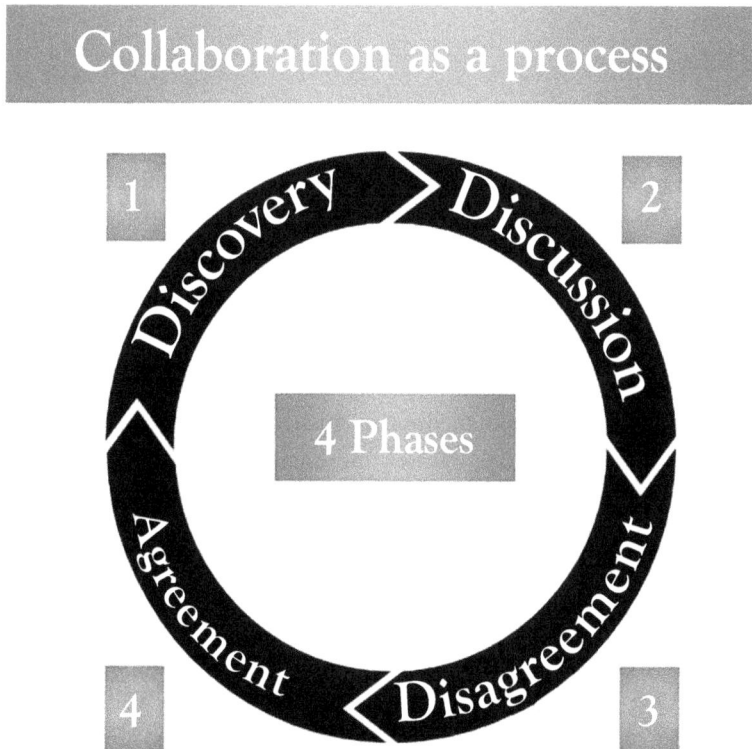

Figure 3.1 The process of collaboration

perspectives, ideas, issues, options, and possibilities. So it is critical to spend sufficient time on the discovery phase without rushing.

Regardless of whether or not one knows the parties already, it is essential to develop rapport and get to know their needs and interests.

There is always something new to be learned about the people in a collaboration, even if they have worked together before.

A common mistake inexperienced collaborators make in the workplace is to assume that they already know their colleagues, so they do not ask essential questions that would enable them to uncover more information about those individuals that can make the collaboration more meaningful and build even stronger partnerships. This is equivalent to walking into a dark tunnel without proper lighting to see the depths of what is already there.

There are three dimensions that are part of the Discovery phase:

1. People
2. Purpose
3. Perceptions

The Discovery phase involves satisfying one's curiosity about the people involved to learn more details about their unique backgrounds, experience, expertise, motivations, and talents. Discovering more about the people beyond the limits of their roles in the collaboration uncovers unique information about each party and is essential to developing empathy, rapport, and trust.

Having a common collaboration purpose that everyone commits to is also a crucial part of the Discovery phase. The key goal is the expected outcome based on a common vision or mission. Asking critical questions can help the team explore, discuss, and identify the collaboration purpose. Examples of some essential questions to ask include:

- Why should there be a collaboration, and for what long-term strategy and purpose?
- What are the impacts if a collaboration does not take place?
- What does a "successful" collaboration look like for you?
- What are the team's core values for the collaboration?
- What innovative ideas, improvements, or changes will the collaboration achieve?

- What makes this specific collaboration unique?
- What will the collaboration achieve that is meaningful?

An important part of the Discovery phase is to allocate sufficient time to make sure there is a mutual understanding about what the key focus of the collaboration will entail: should it be about a past or current problem to resolve, or an opportunity to create for the future? This duality of a problem or an opportunity as the potential focus is well worth spending time to think through and evaluate thoroughly before deciding. Accepting a problem or opportunity at face value without considering the other alternative can result in an unproductive use of time by overlooking critical issues that need to be addressed to achieve the best possible outcomes.

The Discussion phase features a highly interactive exchange of information and ideas about the topic. Key discussion activities include: asking pertinent questions, stating concerns, suggesting ideas, giving and receiving input, conducting research, collecting data, reviewing documentation, and talking about options and alternatives to consider. Since the discussion should be a dialogue and not a monologue with anyone dominating, following an agreed-upon process to ensure active and equal participation is essential. This will help each party feel emotionally safe and secure from conflict or retaliation for anything said. Agreeing to guidelines for how the discussion should be structured also helps achieve maximum input and peak efficiency. For example, not allowing interruptions or questions, while people are speaking, is a time-efficient way to enable the equal exchange of ideas.

Enabling productive dialogues in a collaboration requires a delicate balance of task and relationship behaviors. Strong leadership, to balance task-related activities with ones that maintain positive relationships and trust, is one of the best ways to ensure a highly interactive and comprehensive dialogue. Task behaviors include: asking for clarification, summarizing, following an agenda, giving each person the same amount of time to speak, and referring to a "parking lot" to document questions and topics to address later on. Maintenance behaviors include: acknowledging comments and concerns, encouraging more quiet people to speak up, ensuring confidentiality, and establishing a comfortable and safe emotional climate for open discussion.

Sometimes tensions occur during collaborations due to the individual conflict triggers each party experiences. Each party needs to be self-aware of what triggers conflict reactions and take accountability for the self-management of those triggers to ensure that one does not restrain one's own or others' participation in collaborative discussions.

Managing Disagreement Proactively

How disagreement is both encouraged and managed by the collaborators can either strengthen or weaken the unity of the parties involved. When managed effectively, disagreement can be a positive factor to increase understanding of different ways of thinking to foster increased innovation for change. For disagreement to be constructive, there needs to be an emotional climate of trust, free from risk of retaliation or reprisals from other group members. There also needs to be the common understanding that disagreement is necessary for achieving the collaboration goal.

There are many obstacles to disagreement that involve attitudes and misconceptions, including:

- Perceiving disagreement as a negative trait.
- Thinking that agreement is best.
- Being afraid to say no.
- Overemphasizing consensus.
- Lacking trust among the parties.
- Failing to create and enforce consistent communication processes for managing disagreement constructively.
- Not taking personal accountability for how one's responses during disagreement affect others on the team.
- Thinking and reacting too defensively.

Managing disagreement proactively in a collaboration requires the group's commitment to follow an agreed-upon process to address different opinions openly. A best practice is to ensure that there are "ground rules" for discussion to encourage constructive argumentation. These "ground rules" typically include acceptable group norms for tone, wording, attitudes, intent, listening guidelines, questions to ask to encourage discussion, and methods for giving constructive feedback.

The first step in managing disagreement in collaborations is to identify the level of conflict involved. There are four possible levels, and each one has distinct characteristics, as follows:

1. *Restrained*: The disagreement is carefully controlled, with some subtle signs, such as cautious wording and tense body language.
2. *Emerging*: The disagreement is more obvious with small signs, including: nonverbal signs signaling emotions such as tension, discomfort, or annoyance, and indirect statements hinting at disagreement, but not stating it openly.
3. *Active*: The disagreement is highly visible, but controlled, such as a loud voice, strong body language, and more confident and open statements of disagreement.
4. *Escalated*: The disagreement reaches the highest level of conflict, including threats, aggression, yelling, crying, and other indicators of the strongest possible emotions and negative behaviors.

After identifying the specific conflict level, collaborators can then tailor their approach using proven strategies for that level. For restrained conflict, these strategies are recommended:

- Interview each party individually to learn more about possible causes.
- Refer to the "ground rules" to ensure that people demonstrate the agreed-upon norms and behaviors at all times during disagreement.
- Remind all parties that different opinions are encouraged.
- Appoint a leader or facilitator to monitor the situation and be ready to apply different strategies if the conflict worsens to the emerging level.

During emerging disagreements, these strategies can be very effective:

- Emphasize the importance of tolerating all opinions, even if one does not agree.
- Interview each party individually to identify potential solutions.
- Emphasize the importance of disagreement against the problem, not judgment against the person.
- Facilitate a dialogue to enable each party to state views without interruptions or criticisms.
- Facilitate a question and answer session that focuses on how the opinions relate to the collaboration goal.

For active levels of disagreement, applying the following strategies can help all parties listen actively and stay focused:

- Remind the parties of their need to focus on a common vision or goal and not get sidetracked by differences of opinion.
- Reframe and reintroduce the "ground rules" for disagreement as the means to encourage diverse thinking, and not to polarize the team into competing factions.
- Choose a neutral facilitator to conduct the discussion, giving everyone the chance to participate equally.
- Encourage all parties to depersonalize and concentrate on the common goals of the team.
- Refocus the discussion on guidelines for agreement on the best options or solutions, rather than on the disagreement itself.

Once the disagreement has reached its escalated level of emotion, it is difficult to get others to contribute anything constructively. The best strategies are as follows:

- Give all members a "cooling off" period to ensure that emotions are not at their highest: take a break, or schedule another session for a different date and time.
- Involve all parties in discussing the impacts of the conflict on their team performance and lessons learned that can be applied moving forward to achieve the collaboration goal.

- Assign a facilitator, mediator, or arbitrator to help discuss and negotiate next steps.
- Encourage team members to recognize that the best collaboration outcomes result from listening actively to diverse views, even if disagreement occurs.

The Agreement phase involves finalizing all decisions and confirming the conditions, tactics, roles and responsibilities, deadlines, budget, contractual details, and documentation for a plan of action. By this time, all parties should have voiced their input on any objections and concerns. Moving to the Agreement phase too quickly by assuming it has occurred without any confirmation is a common flaw in a project and deadline-driven business environment. This can lead to blocking crucial opportunities for disagreement to hear diverse perspectives.

So this final phase enables everyone to review and confirm actions, roles and responsibilities, and timelines for follow-up. A best practice is to ensure that all parties agree to specific guidelines for reaching group agreement or mutual understanding. It is also helpful if final decisions and related responsibilities and actions are restated to all members of the collaboration both verbally and in writing.

Summary

Collaborating is a complex communication process requiring careful planning, organizing, structuring, and managing of expectations to achieve success. Being able to recognize the specific component of a collaboration enables better regulation and control of the process, resulting in greater probability of success. There are four phases of any collaboration process that typically occur in sequential order, but sometimes overlap. These collaboration phases are as follows:

- Discovery: Explore purpose, people, and perceptions.
- Discussion: Give and take input and suggestions.
- Disagreement: Address objections and differences proactively.
- Agreement: Finalize decisions, contracts, responsibilities, and actions.

The Discovery phase is an important first step to ensuring that collaborators are sufficiently prepared for what is ahead. This phase has three dimensions of equal importance: people, purpose, and perceptions. Building rapport and trust with the other parties is a priority for this component, as it will establish a strong foundation for withstanding the ups and downs that collaborators experience inevitably. Identifying a common purpose for the collaboration will help the collaborator parties stay focused throughout the entire process. This phase also involves examining both dimensions of the collaboration topic: a past or present problem to resolve, or an opportunity to create in the future.

The Discussion phase involves more than just giving and taking input and suggestions. It also requires setting "ground rules" and implementing systematic methods for communicating openly and honestly with assertiveness and tact. It is paramount to allocate enough time to exchange input from all parties before moving to a decision too fast, before all possible opinions and suggestions are conveyed. Ensuring that there is equal participation through dialogue, instead of some speakers dominating the discussion through a monologue, requires careful management.

Strategies include setting discussion guidelines based on a balance of task-related and relationship-related activities. Some examples of task-related behaviors include: using an agenda, having a "parking lot" of items to address later, and summarizing. Some examples of actions to take to build collaboration team trust and synergy are ensuring confidentiality, acknowledging comments and concerns, and encouraging the quieter people to speak up while not being intimidated or interrupted.

The Disagreement phase involves encouraging as much disagreement as possible. Without disagreement, there is a lack of diverse thinking, and this can limit the quality of ideas, options, and solutions. The four levels of disagreement are restrained, emerging, active, and escalated.

The Agreement phase concentrates primarily on finalizing and documenting all decisions and confirming related actions, roles, and timelines. Restating the terms of agreements both verbally and in writing ensures that there are no misunderstandings or oversights about next actions and responsibilities.

CHAPTER 4

Analyzing Problems and Opportunities Strategically

It is the long history of humankind (and animal kind, too) that those
who learned to collaborate and improvise most effectively have prevailed.
—Charles Darwin

Preview

This chapter discusses the importance of being both adaptable and systematic about determining what to spend time and energy on as a collaboration topic. This means doing the necessary planning to determine if it is best for the collaboration outcome to focus on a problem or an opportunity. In this chapter, a problem is defined as a past or present situation or issue to resolve, and an opportunity is featured as a future possibility to create. Each, problem or opportunity, requires different thinking styles and communication approaches for the most efficient and effective collaboration outcomes.

Having a Clear Collaboration Focus: Problem or Opportunity?

A major risk to the results of a collaboration is to accept the topic at face value and rush to finalize the tactical details of who, what, when, where, and how. This approach can lead one to the path of failure. The surest path to success is to begin by analyzing the collaboration topic framework as either a problem or an opportunity, and then to choose what is best for the collaboration goals and outcomes overall. Focusing strategically on the big picture of how the collaboration topic is to be reframed helps ensure that the collaboration parties spend their energy and time most productively.

The first step is to view the collaboration topic from the double lens of both a problem and an opportunity. Whereas a problem is a past or present situation or occurrence that has to be resolved, an opportunity is a future reality that can be created.

Each one, a problem or an opportunity, requires a different thinking approach, time allocation, structure, and discussion emphasis. Attempting to address a problem and an opportunity simultaneously, in the same way, with a one-size-fits-all solution, only serves to diminish the quality of the discussion and can impede the results significantly(Table 4.1).

Table 4.1 Planning collaborations strategically: Topic focus

Problem	Opportunity
Past or present focus	Future focus
Analyzing causes and effects for context more	Investigating ideas, motivations, and innovations as possibilities
Narrow down details	Broaden one's perspective
Organize in a logical and linear sequence	Organize ideas in a random sequence
What, why, why not, risks and gains?	What, who, how, concepts, exploration of "what if?"
Goal is resolving	Goal is creating

Asking Relevant Questions

Knowing what questions to ask that are most relevant to either a problem or an opportunity is essential for the most productive and effective team discussions. Problem solving effectively requires sufficient time to discuss all contextual information about the data and facts. The problem must also be analyzed in-depth: is it a symptom or the underlying cause? Collaborations that focus on a problem usually involve extensive discussion and disagreement about the methodology and solutions to be considered or tested, before agreement can occur. In comparison, opportunity-focused collaborations typically concentrate more on inventing options based on idea generation than on facts.

For example, a collaboration based on resolving a problem would typically involve analytical questions about the causes, effects, and context of a past or current problem before attempting to explore innovative solutions. In contrast, the questions that would typically be asked in an opportunity-based collaboration involve less focus on the past or current context, and more speculation about possibilities for the future. The following are examples of relevant questions to ask about a collaboration problem:

- What is the apparent problem?
- Is it really the problem, or is it a symptom of a deeper root cause?
- What is the context of the problem: background, users and stakeholders, assumptions, causes, and pertinent information?
- What is the supporting data and related research?
- What has been done in the past to resolve the same or similar problems?
- What systems, policies, and procedures are currently involved?
- How effective are these systems, policies, and procedures in resolving the problem?
- What specific actions need to take place to resolve the problem?
- What are some innovative solutions that would resolve the problem?
- What are the requested or required timelines to resolve the problem?
- How will results be measured?
- Is a collaboration the best way to resolve the problem?

The previous questions draw attention to the need to gain more context about the problem, including root cause analysis, and related systems, policies, procedures, and resolutions. In contrast, the questions for an opportunity-based collaboration are typically more concerned about investigating ideas, motivations, and innovations as possibilities than about analyzing the concrete data and facts to support them.

Some examples of typical questions about a collaboration opportunity include:

- What is the perceived opportunity?

- What are other related opportunities?
- Which opportunity is the best to consider?
- What are the benefits of pursuing the opportunity?
- What are the risks if the opportunity is not pursued?
- What are some current ideas that can be adapted for the opportunity?
- What are some upcoming future trends in innovation that should be considered?
- What is the supporting data and research?
- What are some new ideas that can be invented for the opportunity?
- Suppose you are one of the stakeholders or end users:
  o What would motivate you about this opportunity?
  o What would demotivate you about this opportunity?
- What really excites you about this opportunity?
- Is a collaboration the best way to address this opportunity?

Framing the Discussion Strategically

Making a collective decision about how to reframe the collaboration topic can be challenging because not everyone will have the same thinking style, knowledge, or level of interest. Some people will prefer focusing on the problem since it is easy for them to think that way if they are extremely analytical, or perhaps due to habit based on their current role. Other collaborators will prefer exploring the topic as an opportunity because they are used to this type of thinking on the job, or they find it more interesting personally. So it is important for all parties to be open-minded about the benefits and drawbacks of investing time on a problem or an opportunity, and to agree collectively on which topic emphasis they believe will be the best way to achieve their goal.

Once the collaborators have agreed on the big picture strategy for the topic focus, they will need to decide how to manage the discussion process. Collaborations with a problem-solution focus tend to need a logical and linear structure to organize the content and format systematically. Some ways to tailor the structure for a problem-based collaboration include:

- Establish time limits for each participant's input to reduce information overload.
- Enforce "ground rules" for discussion-only segments without interruptions or debates.
- State the problem to address at each meeting to keep all parties focused.
- Follow a process for decision making based on specific criteria.
- Include "lessons learned" at the end of each session to encourage risk-taking.

Structuring opportunity-focused collaborations most effectively can be accomplished in the following ways:

- Communicate the opportunity at the beginning of each session to stay focused.
- Keep idea-generating sessions separate from discussions involving disagreement about executional details and logistics.
- Reduce the scope of agendas to allow more time for flexibility and spontaneity.
- Include spontaneous, polychronic time segments: relaxed, unstructured, no specific timelines, and no watching the clock.
- Encourage tolerance of ambiguity during idea generation and discussion segments to avoid moving to solutions and actions too fast.

There are some common strategies for managing discussion and disagreement that apply to both problem-based and opportunity-based collaborations. Initially, there needs to be a clear set of expectations about relationship norms for behavior that enable discussions to be constructive without becoming defensive or blame-oriented. This includes how to deal with interruptions, negative comments, and dominating or aggressive behaviors. It helps to address how some of these behaviors will be managed throughout the collaboration process by establishing and enforcing "ground rules". Some examples of common phrases for "ground rules" to unite all parties to support each other include: "one team, one voice," "*us* against the problem, not *you* are the problem," and "discussion does not need agreement or disagreement." Sometimes it is best to restrict comments or questions until everyone has had the chance to state their views. To achieve this end, all parties should understand the difference between a "discussion" to share ideas and "disagreement" to provide argumentation about why or why not?

Additional strategies for achieving strategic alignment within the group to achieve constructive discussions about the topic include:

1. Ensure that the leader or facilitator remains "neutral" during discussions and disagreements.
2. Avoid getting sidetracked during discussions and record ideas for later on in a "Parking Lot" list.
3. Prepare the group for handling disagreement by encouraging everyone to take the first step by expressing their views openly regarding small issues of little relevance, such as when to take breaks, or how to improve a meeting process.
4. Conduct informal surveys for participants to self-assess how well the group manages its own discussion and disagreement, and is able to implement some of its own suggestions.
5. Provide training in conflict management, critical thinking, and problem solving to help those individuals who lead and facilitate discussions and disagreements to acquire new methods and techniques.

Specific strategies for managing discussion and disagreement in problem-based collaborations include:

1. Create a group list of standardized questions to ask during discussions and disagreements, such as "how will that method address the problem?" and "what are the possible risks and gains of that solution?"
2. Ask for commitment to prioritize the problem and solution first, and egos and personal agendas last.
3. Utilize subgroups to share ideas and concerns with each other and then summarize a few for the entire team.

4. Reframe and paraphrase comments to align them with the collaboration goal and the problem to address, so the discussion does not lose focus.

5. Ensure that when others challenge an idea, methodology, or solution, they are hard on the problem, not the person.

For managing discussion and disagreement in opportunity-based collaborations, recommended strategies are as follows:

1. Get commitment that during idea-generating discussions, any concerns about the present realities of budget, resources, deadlines, and other practical details will be deferred to a "Parking Lot" list to address at a more suitable time.

2. Encourage conveying concepts and ideas in creative ways other than words, such as with drawings, photos, illustrations, diagrams, and other visuals that engage all of the senses to be most creative during brainstorming.

3. Encourage the group to use exploratory and speculative language such as "imagine that," or "suppose…," or "what if we considered doing …?" to make discussing possibilities feel open, safe, secure, and noncommittal.

4. Remind the group about their commitment to take ownership of all ideas together, to avoid self-promotion or overselling individual ideas.

5. Emphasize disagreement as a way to make the opportunities better for all, rather than criticizing individuals for their ideas.

Some recommendations for structuring problem-based collaborations include: limiting time for each participant to speak to avoid information overload, stating the problem at each session to stay focused, and addressing "lessons learned" at the end of each meeting to emphasize continuous improvement and encourage risk-taking and innovation. For opportunity-based collaborations, ways to provide structure most effectively include: communicating the opportunity at each session to stay focused, reduce the scope of agendas to enable time for spontaneity and flexibility, and include polychronic time segments that are spontaneous and unstructured to encourage a relaxed pace without imposing time limits for expressing and exploring creative ideas.

Summary

Having a clear strategy for the purpose and goal of a collaboration is the first step to success. Before getting too caught up in the details of a collaboration, it is essential to determine its key purpose: to resolve a problem or to explore an opportunity. Whereas a problem-based collaboration is based on resolving a past or current problem, an opportunity-based collaboration concentrates more on a future state of possibilities.

When managing discussion and disagreement in a problem-based collaboration, some specific strategies include:

- Assign the group a task to create standardized questions to ask.
- Paraphrase or reframe comments to align with the problem and the discussion goal to avoid losing focus.
- Be hard on the problem, and not overly critical of the person.

For opportunity-based collaborations, key strategies that work well for managing discussion and disagreement are as follows:

- Ensure that when generating ideas for the future, any comments about the realities of the present, such as budget, deadlines, or resources, will be deferred to a "Parking Lot" list until a more suitable time.
- Encourage input in more than just words, including: photos, drawings, diagrams, illustrations, and other visuals that engage all of the senses for effective brainstorming.
- Discourage self-promotion of ideas and encourage group ownership and accountability instead.

CHAPTER 5

Negotiating to Influence Decisions in Collaborations

A clear purpose will unite you as you move forward, values will guide your behavior, and goals will focus your energy.
—Kenneth H. Blanchard

Preview

This chapter discusses effective strategies that enable successful negotiating and decision making in any type of collaboration. These strategies are aligned to one of three negotiating skill categories, as follows:

- Questioning: Uncovering different perspectives.
- Messaging: Constructing messages systematically.
- Persuading: Communicating influentially for commitment.

All of these skills are crucial in a collaboration for achieving others' buy-in and commitment to approve ideas and streamline decision making. The first skill category, effective questioning, focuses on the importance of meaningful inquiry to learn more about others' viewpoints nonjudgmentally. The second skill category, deliberate messaging, pertains to planning one's message by choosing words carefully. The final skill category entails the essential principles and practices of persuasion, including acknowledging, reframing, neutralizing, and empathizing.

Asking Meaningful Questions

Preparing and asking thoughtful questions to learn more about others' perspectives, needs, and concerns is an important secret to achieving

Table 5.1 Influencing decisions by questioning

12 Key Question Types when Collaborating			
1	Realty Check: for understanding key issues and processes	7	Suppose: "What if" to generate ideas for the future
2	Hypothetical: Imagine you are in their place	8	Open-ended: Answer generally with the possibility of more than two options
3	Emotional Thermometer: Comfort Level?	9	Closed-ended: Answer specifically based on only two options, such as "yes" or "no"
4	Implications and Impacts?	10	Rhetorical: Ask without expecting an answer to stimulate thinking
5	Trial Balloon: How close to deciding?	11	Confirmation: Double check before deciding
6	Leading: Getting them to admit a concern or risk	12	Reflective: Self-awareness and lessons learned

success as a collaborator. Neglecting to ask meaningful questions that engage others to reveal more about themselves can limit the potential to reach a mutually-satisfying agreement among all collaboration parties. The art of questioning in a collaboration requires effective planning and special communication skills, especially assertiveness, active listening, tact, and empathy. Successful collaborators are able to employ a variety of questions with deliberate intent.

There are 12 types of questions that are particularly suitable to ask when negotiating and decision making in a collaboration (Table 5.1).

The following list identifies each question type with a real-life example:

1. *Reality check:* What is your understanding of the new process?
2. *Hypothetical:* Suppose you are one of our nontechnical customers. What do you think would be some specific challenges you might face as a customer when attempting to use that specific software application?
3. *Emotional thermometer:* How comfortable do you feel about implementing that option in your organization?
4. *Implications:* How do you think this will affect the safety of your staff?

5. *Trial balloon:* Would you consider conducting a test program with us, assuming we can agree on the budget today?

6. *Leading:* So, based on what I have heard you say, are you concerned that without the political support of our board of directors, this option might be at risk for failure?

7. *Suppose:* What do you envision would be some of the advantages over the current system if we used that approach instead to track customer complaints?

8. *Open-ended:* What are your concerns about that option?

9. *Closed-ended:* So do we all agree that this is our first priority?

10. *Rhetorical:* Aren't we brilliant as a collaboration team?

11. *Confirmation:* How can we be sure that there will be no additional costs involved?

12. *Reflective*: If you reflect on that conversation with the Board of Directors, what were your lessons learned, and what will you think about and do differently next time?

Messaging: Choosing Words Deliberately

When negotiating in a collaboration, word choices can make a big difference concerning whether or not the end result is a success or a failure. Words have the power to cause either tension and confusion or trust and understanding. Words that are aggressive, imprecise, or unclear can create serious communication problems, including defensiveness, confusion, information gaps, conflicts, and delayed decision making. When selecting words for influencing others effectively in a collaboration, following the guidelines below will help ensure peak results:

- Choose "We" and "Us" instead of "I" to emphasize partnership. Example: The key question is, "What are we going to do about it to make things better for all of us?"
- Say "And" instead of "But" and "However" after expressing empathy. Example: "I understand this is a busy time *and* . . . ."
- Choose tentative language. Example: "Suppose…," "what do you think about…?," "if…, then perhaps we can …."

- Focus on the goal. Examples: "So do you think this modification will help us achieve our goal?" and "I am concerned that this option will not fully support the goal of this negotiation."

Leveraging the Principles of Persuasion

Since negotiating is a deliberate and structured process for persuasion, understanding how to leverage the principles of influence in a collaboration using a methodical approach is crucial for achieving optimal results. An efficient process for putting persuasion into practice is the "PARTNER" method, explained as follows:

P rovide honest input with transparency for all.

A cknowledge the individual and mutual interests involved.

R eframe suggestions and objections based on how they affect the collaboration goal.

T one should be confident, sincere, and respectful.

N eutralize using objective, nonemotional words.

E mpathize, don't criticize.

R esponsibility and accountability are key.

The "PARTNER" approach involves seven steps, and it begins with the first step of agreement to participate actively in the collaboration by being honest and open with feedback. Transparency is necessary to ensure ethical practices and build trust.

Acknowledgment is the second step in the "PARTNER" method. Acknowledging what is driving the discussion and decision making enables the collaborator to gain invaluable insights about the other party's underlying motivations and concerns. Examples of interests are the need to be more productive, and the intent to reduce financial risks. Acknowledgment is a way of letting the other party know that one's interest in what is being said is meaningful to one or all concerned. It also grounds the conversation to emphasize a common connection between the collaboration parties to establish that what is said is being listened to intently, is recognized, and is valued.

Examples of 10 common interests that drive what people say, care about, argue over, and decide in a collaboration include:

1. Recognition: personal or professional. This is the need to receive credit for what one achieves in one's life or work. Feeling that one is genuinely being appreciated and valued for one's worth, skills, and accomplishments are key aspects of this self-motivation.

2. Security: emotional, financial, and physical. This can include shelter, acceptance, money, and mental and physical well-being. Some specific examples of this self-motivation are the need for job security, financial security, family security, feeling safe in one's surroundings, and being protected from harm.

3. Growth: acquiring more knowledge and experience. Usually this self-motivation involves a readiness for change of some kind. An interest in growth can involve aspects that are financial, intellectual, emotional, and physical.

4. Pride: in oneself or others, based on self-worth or accomplishments. This relates to feelings of worthiness and can also instill optimism in self or others, or pride in attaining a goal or developing a team.

5. Acceptance: by self and others. Accepting one's strengths and weaknesses can build the confidence to assume accountability, despite the risks involved. Acceptance from others can also help build self-confidence that can lead to increased rapport and trust.

6. Fear: of consequences and impacts. Fear is not only a negative response; it can be positive motivation for taking risks to support change to make the future better.

7. Independence: to be able to decide on one's own how to think and act. It means wanting independence of thought and action based on having individual freedom and autonomy.

8. Curiosity: to explore, experiment, and understand. One of the most underestimated of the self-motivators, being curious about unknown places and experiences can be a very positive incentive to take accountability for exploring an idea or application that is unique, new, and different.

9. Status: political, social, and professional prestige, influence, and power. Wanting to achieve a higher status can motivate people to accept opportunities that offer them this potential, despite the risks.

10. Fulfillment: self-gratification that a requirement, promise, or goal will be realized, causing one to feel satisfaction about achieving that end.

According to Beth Harvey, Senior Manager, Global Procurement, knowing the other party well in terms of their interests, and leveraging that knowledge is key to negotiating success. Beth identifies additional strategies that work especially well when collaborating with the internal negotiation team in preparation for negotiating with vendors or suppliers. These include: meeting in advance to be clear about roles and responsibilities; developing a fact-based negotiations strategy based on market, industry, price, potential risks, and other pertinent influences; agreeing to a list of "must-haves" to predetermine one's position and threshold for each; and negotiating at your own location for a competitive advantage.[1]

Reframing Is Key

Another way to achieve success when negotiating in a collaboration is to revise one's wording to refocus the messaging. This is known as "reframing." Selecting the right words can create a positive tone, increase trust, clarify meanings, resolve differences, and inspire accountability. Posing a question, such as, "Tell me how that change will help us achieve the goal?" is one way to reframe. Another reframing technique when negotiating is to reword what was said, based on the collaboration goal or common interest. For example, one can reframe a mutual interest by saying, "I would like to know how you envision this delay affecting our goal of providing our customers with a more seamless approach to using our software for these products and services." In this case, making the customer approach seamless is the common interest that is, in essence, the reframed word "hook" intended to have the strongest influence on the other party.

---

[1] Harvey, Beth, Senior Manager, Global Procurement. 2019 (September 1, November 13). E-mail messages to author.

Another critical aspect of reframing is to convey a positive tone. The tone should be assertive and confident, not overbearing or self-righteous. There are many ways to convey a confident tone without overdoing it. One approach is to select words that end in upward vocal inflections, such as "yes," "I agree," and "another way." As well, citing data and facts to respond diplomatically and nondefensively to objections, such as, "ninety-percent of our customers disagree with that option," makes it clear that one is confident about one's point. Being sincere about objecting by stating it matter-of-factly without the need to make it a personal attack on someone also creates a climate where disagreement can occur without blame or retaliation.

A different way to reframe is to eliminate emotionally loaded, hot language. This is called neutralizing. Some critics might misinterpret neutralizing as sugarcoating words to be too polite or superficial. However, when it is done well, neutralizing is a very tactful way to depersonalize and encourage dialogue, especially in heated conflict situations. Although neutralizing takes some practice to edit wording quickly, there are some ways to accomplish it efficiently in a group setting. The first way is to require the collaboration parties to follow specific "ground rules" for how objections are worded to neutralize discussion when it becomes heated. For example, instead of saying, "that is a terrible idea and it will never work," one can say, "I believe that was tried before and the results we are looking for were not achieved using that technique." Rather than stating, "*You* are wrong," saying, "I am not sure about the accuracy of that information" challenges the statement instead of criticizing and blaming the person unnecessarily. Another way to neutralize is to rephrase what the person said in nonemotional, objective language to express one's understanding. For instance, if a collaborator says, "You aren't listening and you always do that," you can say, "I know I need to listen better and I will not interrupt you. Please continue."

A simple way to reframe words to be more objective and less personal or accusatory is to replace personal pronouns before nouns with articles, such as "the," "a," or "an," resulting in avoiding too much personalization. For example, instead of saying, "This responsibility is an important part of *your* job," simply changing one small word to say, "This responsibility is an important part of *the* job" conveys a more neutral message and tone.

Failure to neutralize one's message can result in misunderstandings, defensiveness, conflict, escalation of complaints upwards to senior leaders, and derailed conversations. The following chart illustrates simple examples of how to edit specific words to neutralize the message in a conversation to achieve influencing power in a collaboration:

Instead of	Say
My request	The request
Your problem	A problem
Let's discuss your objections…	Let's discuss the key issues…
Senior Management decided that you are	It was agreed that your skills are
I believe this is a good opportunity for you to…	This project offers an opportunity to …
You should be aware that …	The situation is that…
I would like your agreement…	Agreeing to this opportunity will…
If you do not take accountability…	Taking accountability means…

Although these changes appear to be minor, they can make a big difference in establishing a meaningful dialogue that emphasizes "us against the business problem" without any possible misinterpretation about the message being "you are the problem."

Empathy is the next-to-the-last letter in "PARTNER" and its importance cannot be exaggerated. Empathy is often easier to talk about than to demonstrate. Despite good intentions, strong emotions can sometimes hinder one's ability to feel or show empathy in those tough moments when self-preservation and self-interest tend to dominate. While someone is talking, it takes tremendous discipline to slow down one's brain from skipping ahead to think about contradictions, exceptions, questions, and differing points of view.

Demonstrating empathy requires a positive mindset and intent, and the patience to listen actively without judgment. Empathy originates with thinking "and" instead of "but." Thinking and saying "and" is the best approach when one's objective is to convey to another person that you heard what was said and your empathy is authentic, not fake. The word "and" represents a collaborative mindset that is highly cooperative in wanting to hear other points of view without being dismissive. The word "but" is effective when emphasizing objections, such as "I agree with that, but..." The downside is that the "but" can also shut down a conversation by contradicting any initial empathy and making it appear to sound insincere. Other wording alternatives to "and" include "so" and "also." If eliminating "but" is especially challenging, try ending the sentence, pausing before continuing to the next sentence.

Some people ask if "however" or "although" are better options. In fact, these two words should also be avoided if one's goal is to show empathy. For example, saying, "I know you are concerned about the date, however…." appears to contradict the empathy.

Imagine trying to influence someone to comply with a policy by saying, "I know you have concerns, *but* there is no other choice than to take responsibility for that …." Since this statement uses "but" after the empathy part, there is the potential for the receiver to interpret the empathy as fake. It would be better to say, "I know you have concerns, *and* I really want to truly understand them from your perspective."

The final step in "PARTNER" is ensuring responsibility and accountability between both parties. There are some ways to motivate others to take accountability for delivering on their promises and be responsible for meeting key obligations and deadline dates. Some of the ways to accomplish this include:

1. Agree on key milestones for key accomplishments and ways to achieve them most efficiently.
2. Provide coaching and mentoring to develop essential skills for peak performance.
3. Encourage networking with other collaboration parties to share expertise and resources.
4. Schedule separate meetings to discuss challenges and obstacles and ways to overcome them.
5. Create a plan for knowledge sharing and transfer to develop shared ownership as a collaboration team.

Summary

This chapter discusses essential strategies that enable successful negotiating and decision making in any type of collaboration. These strategies apply to one of three key skill categories, as follows:

- Questioning: Uncovering different perspectives.
- Messaging: Constructing messages systematically.
- Persuading: Communicating influentially for commitment.

Key ways to build strong partnerships in a collaboration are asking meaningful questions, reframing messages, especially through careful word choice, neutralizing emotional responses, and maintaining a positive tone. There are 12 types of questions that can help uncover and encourage different perspectives include the following:

1. Reality check
2. Hypothetical
3. Emotional thermometer
4. Implications
5. Trial balloon
6. Leading
7. Suppose
8. Open-ended
9. Closed-ended
10. Rhetorical
11. Confirmation
12. Reflective

Taking the "PARTNER" approach enables collaborators to follow a proven process for negotiating and influencing other parties with assertiveness and tact. The "PARTNER" approach includes seven steps for reframing the message to be both assertive and tactful:

P rovide honest input with transparency to help make things better for all concerned.

A cknowledge the individual or mutual interests involved.

R eframe suggestions and objections based on the collaboration goal.

T one should be confident, sincere, and respectful.

N eutralize using objective, nonemotional words.

E mpathize, don't criticize.

R esponsibility and accountability are key.

CHAPTER 6

Navigating Conflict When Collaborating

Whenever you're in conflict with someone, there is one factor that can make the difference between damaging your relationship and deepening it. That factor is your attitude.

—William James

Preview

The first step when collaborating is to accept that encountering conflict is inevitable for any collaborator, so making a conscious effort to become more comfortable with conflict is the best way to ensure success. By demonstrating conflict management strategies consistently, collaborators can increase their effectiveness when conflict does occur.

This chapter focuses on two aspects of navigating conflict successfully when collaborating: first, the self-management of one's own conflict reactions, and second, managing others' conflict responses and behaviors proactively. Applying self-awareness and self-control emotionally, physiologically, and intellectually helps to increase one's individual agility and resiliency significantly during conflicts. The most proactive step in self-awareness is to identify and manage one's conflict trigger responses before they escalate.

Becoming more observant of others' responses and then adapting one's communication approach, especially by demonstrating assertiveness and tact, is the best way to navigate conflict. This chapter explains proven communication strategies for adapting during conflict situations in a collaboration, including: setting expectations, addressing objections, managing team dynamics, and delivering constructive messages to address and resolve critical issues.

Self-Managing Conflict Responses

Seasoned collaborators know a best-kept secret to effective collaboration, namely that conflict is something to cultivate, not avoid. Collaborators who are able to disagree openly and honestly benefit potentially from hearing more diverse approaches, decisions, and results. Although conflict can be uncomfortable, if managed well, it can also serve as a catalyst that transforms disagreements into discussions about options and solutions that are outstanding due to blending differing perspectives and areas of expertise.

Taking a systematic approach to managing one's own conflict responses enables collaborators to identify root causes efficiently and apply appropriate strategies situationally. The first step in this process is to increase one's self-awareness and self-control on these three levels (Table 6.1):

1. Emotional
2. Physiological
3. Cognitive

Table 6.1 Self-managing conflict responses

Awareness	Emotional	Physiological	Cognitive
Level 1 (lowest)	Identify conflict triggers	Identify physical reactions to conflict	Identify one's perception of conflict
Level 2	Explore ways to control one's responses	Explore how to control or treat those reactions	Explore negative perceptions of conflict
Level 3 (highest)	Change one's responses when "triggered"	Become more proactive in addressing physiological responses	Become more comfortable with conflict

Addressing the Emotional Level

The emotional level of conflict is challenging for anyone to handle, but self-awareness combined with self-control can make the experience easier. The secret is to recognize early when one is affected personally, or "triggered," by conflict, and identify as specifically as possible what feelings are involved. The emotional responses from conflict can be conscious or unconscious reactions. Some examples of emotional responses include fear, frustration, anger, impatience, uncertainty, defensiveness, and avoidance. Examples of being "triggered" by conflict include:

- Feeling upset by a raised voice tone.
- Becoming tense when watching someone stand up, slam the door, and storm out of a room.
- Being afraid to confront someone with a different opinion.
- Experiencing anxiety while watching two people yelling at each other.
- Withdrawing from an argument due to feeling overwhelmed.

Physiological Responses

Once collaborators identify their own emotional reactions to conflict, they should be mindful of the physiological responses they experience as a result. Examples of physiological responses to conflict include rapid heart rate, sweating, increased adrenaline, tightening of one's vocal cords, nausea, and digestive issues, to name a few. These biological reactions occur automatically when the body attempts to defend itself from real or perceived harm. For self-protection, and also by force of habit, individuals typically respond to conflict in one of two ways: fight or flight.

An example of a fight response is when one gets angry and frustrated at the other for not taking accountability. Often people with fight responses have a highly assertive nature with an action focus. This can cause them to be very forceful and vocal at times when communicating their needs. People with fight tendencies during conflict are inclined to have a strong determination to press for agreement from others quickly and take action, often overlooking the need to spend sufficient time building trust first.

The flight trigger is another defensive response. It is based on wanting to withdraw. Individuals exhibiting this response typically seek to avoid or delay being assertive due to fear of causing more tension and conflict during disagreement. Perhaps they want to make sure they have acquired all the facts, or they do not want to risk communicating too forcefully. Although the motivations for avoidance are justifiable, other parties could perceive this response as being weak, noncommittal, or indifferent when, in fact, it is more likely to be a self-preservation tactic.

If the flight trigger is suppressed over an extended period of time, it can escalate into a passive-aggressive response based on feelings of helplessness, powerlessness, anger, or resentment. This type of reaction is also a defense mechanism and typically involves the open venting of negative feelings and thoughts that have accumulated over time. Individuals who demonstrate a passive-aggressive response are often "triggered" by a perceived loss of power or control over a situation that builds gradually until they feel compelled to release their pent-up feelings and express them bluntly.

Taking Action to Manage One's Responses

By recognizing and understanding their own conflict response tendencies, collaborators can progress beyond self-awareness to self-management. Self-managing one's response to conflict is a deliberate mental process that examines the root causes of how one perceives conflict and attempts to overcome these obstacles proactively. The following seven steps are recommended to remain calm and focused during tense conflict situations during a collaboration:

1. Become more self-aware of one's conflict triggers early by learning to notice very small signs before they increase in frequency and severity.
2. Analyze the source of the trigger, and seek to manage one's reactions to it better.
3. Recognize the emotions involved, and practice stress management techniques to minimize the emotional impacts.
4. Discuss the trigger with others to get their advice and help to self-manage it with confidence.
5. Apply cognitive management techniques to self-manage the response, such as creative visualization, meditation, and positive self-talk.
6. Concentrate on not taking others' comments and reactions too personally.
7. Take a mental or physical break as needed to energize and depersonalize.
8. Reframe the conversation to focus on a more objective collaboration goal or outcome.

Reckoning With One's Attitudes Regarding Conflict

To become most effective and resilient, it is essential that collaborators recognize that how they view conflict can significantly affect how well or poorly they deal with it. One's cognitive perceptions of conflict are shaped by many factors in one's life well before a collaboration takes place. These attitudes can originate from personal and cultural perceptions, beliefs, and values one is exposed to in one's childhood and family life. For example, one individual who comes from a family or culture that views conflict as something to avoid might consider conflict a negative force to be reckoned with. As a result, if that individual observes others raise their voices in a discussion, he or she could become uncomfortable and possibly view their discussion as a detrimental form of conflict. In contrast, another individual, who grew up in a family environment that encouraged conflict as a healthy way to vent feelings, might consider a discussion with loud voices as less threatening, and as a natural way to enable open disagreement that will, eventually, create a more positive and meaningful outcome.

It is important to note that not everyone's cognitive views of conflict conform to the traditional values they experienced as children. In some instances, individuals' mindsets about conflict are affected more by their own personalities than their upbringing. For instance, someone who is quiet and introverted might not feel comfortable interrupting others during a discussion, preferring to withdraw during a heated argument. In contrast, an extravert might not mind interruptions so much, and might even become stimulated by loud and open disagreement.

Managing Team Conflicts Constructively

Individuals who can manage their own emotional, physiological, and cognitive conflict responses proactively with self-awareness tend to withstand the many team conflicts during collaborations with optimal resiliency. There are three key strategies that work well for navigating conflicts with team members during all phases of a collaboration. The first strategy is to discuss and agree on expectations for acceptable and unacceptable team norms for behavior during times of tension and disagreement. Having a discussion about norms enables group members to demonstrate their commitment to support and encourage individual differences of opinions in an emotionally safe setting. Specific examples of how to apply this strategy successfully are listed as follows:

- Agree on "ground rules" for how the parties will disagree and decide. This includes:
  o Wording guidelines (e.g., avoid blaming words, like, "your idea is horrible").
  o Group behavior norms (e.g., how interruptions will be managed).
  o Processes (e.g., how final decisions will be made, including voting or the leader having the final say).
- Appoint an internal or external meeting facilitator to ensure that group "ground rules" for disagreement are followed consistently.
- Get commitment from the more assertive members to avoid dominating discussions, so that other less assertive parties can contribute their views equally.

The second strategy to facilitate effective conflict management within collaboration teams is to identify the conflict stage in each situation, and then apply appropriate tactics to manage that stage. The four stages of conflict typically occur in sequence and can be identified as follows:

1. Dormant
2. Emerging
3. Active
4. Aftermath

The Dormant stage is the initial sign of conflict. It involves hidden issues that are not yet visible to others. Typically, during this stage, there are no negative words spoken, and there are no outward signs of disagreement. But if one looks more closely, there are some signs of restraint, such as two individuals never sitting next to each other, strained voice tones, or tense body language.

The Emerging stage is when others' defensive reactions to conflict become a little easier to observe. These responses include more obvious physical demonstrations of discomfort, such as tension, sarcasm, or a blunt statement of disagreement. During this stage, some of those in disagreement can attempt to seek allies supporting their own opinions, and cliques can develop that are based on an "us against them" approach that is passive-aggressive and not constructive.

The Active stage is when the conflict intensity reaches its peak level, so others can observe the responses most easily. Individuals who tend to have a "fight" response become more emotional and vocal during this stage. They can display physical and emotional outbursts, such as slamming doors, yelling, or crying. These interactions can be a battleground of hurt egos, anger, detachment, and nonproductive conversations. There can be in-fighting, criticizing, blaming, and extensive misunderstandings.

In contrast, individuals with "flight" tendencies during conflict will show signs of avoidance, withdrawal, anxiety, and extreme discomfort when they experience or observe conflict. Some people with "flight" responses will politely leave the scene of the conflict, or show other signs of withdrawal, such as minimizing eye contact, or declining to respond to challenging comments and questions. This "flight" response can cause alienation and erode trust between collaboration parties.

If the conflict is resolved, there is an Aftermath stage when all parties experience the effects of what has occurred. Perhaps some individuals will be relieved that the conflict is over and resort to their usual behaviors, whereas other individuals might retreat for some alone time as they attempt to recover from the emotions they either observed or experienced. Regardless of individual reactions, this is a period of recovery for those parties involved directly, as well as those who witnessed the conflict.

Applying Strategies for Each Stage

For the Dormant stage of conflict, the following strategies are recommended.

Strategies for Dormant Stage:

1. Remind all parties that expressing different ideas and concerns openly is necessary for a successful collaboration.

2. Arrange for the group leader or facilitator to meet with each individual confidentially to find out if there are any personal concerns or issues that need to be addressed.

3. Ask a neutral or third party to observe group dynamics and recommend specific actions to take.

During the Emerging stage of conflict, those individuals involved begin to show their discomfort or disagreement both verbally and non-verbally. There is the possibility that "metatalk" will occur, which is when the words stated contradict the body language demonstrated. An example of metatalk is when a collaborator says, "I do not have any objections to that," but frowns and crosses his arms to indicate nonverbal discomfort.

The following strategies are recommended to address and manage conflict during the Emerging stage:

Strategies for Emerging Stage:

1. Meet individually with all group members to discuss concerns and needs.

2. Consider that if only a small percentage of the total collaboration team is involved, meet with those individuals separately to discuss issues, concerns, and proposed solutions before addressing the entire group.

3. Remind the group that disagreement can lead to new ways of thinking and more innovation, and encourage an open discussion about concerns.

4. Reinforce the "ground rules" and group norms for disagreement to ensure a "safe" environment for discussion and constructive input from all parties.

5. Include the issue or concern on the next meeting agenda to discuss then, after team members have had time to think about it and prepare well.

6. Remind the group that disagreement can lead to new ways of thinking and more innovation, so it is important to have open discussion about any concerns.

In the Active stage of conflict, opinions and related emotions are all out in the open. When strong disagreement is vocalized, the group can become divided. Some individuals might seek alliances to support their own interests or political affiliations, and adversarial subgroups can potentially emerge. During this stage when there is so much active disagreement, it is critical to maintain a strong emotional climate of trust that encourages the group to remain unified despite differences. The following strategies are recommended to navigate conflict during this most active stage of open disagreement:

Strategies for Active Phase:

1. Appoint a "neutral" leader or facilitator to solicit constructive input for discussion.
2. Get individual and group commitment to follow the "ground rules" and group norms for behavior.
3. Ensure that the "ground rules" and group norms are identified clearly.
4. Visualize key points and areas of agreement and disagreement within the group, to help everyone remain focused on constructive comments only.
5. Ensure sufficient time for less vocal parties to convey their views as well.
6. Meet in person when possible to maintain unity and build trust.
7. Restrict the use of too much written documentation, such as overuse of e-mails and social media, to minimize conflict escalation.
8. Reframe the focus of the discussion on the collaboration vision, mission, and goal.
9. Summarize and paraphrase points frequently.
10. Document points to refer to afterwards for clarity and understanding.
11. Encourage members to ask questions to uncover underlying motivations, risks, and gains to emphasize the group collaboration goal as the primary focus.
12. Agree on decision-making guidelines that support the collaboration goal.
13. Schedule sufficient time for team members to process the comments intellectually and emotionally before responding or making any decisions.

14. Avoid pressuring the collaboration parties to reach agreement prematurely.

The Aftermath stage is especially important in a collaboration because it offers a unique opportunity for the group to re-establish their trust and consolidate their relationships. Since each individual will experience different postconflict reactions, it is crucial for the team as a unit to re-establish trust, assess how they managed the conflict, and identify action steps for continuous improvement when future conflicts do occur. Conflict strategies for the Aftermath stage are identified as follows:

Strategies for Aftermath Stage:

1. Vocalize and summarize initial concerns and suggestions immediately after the conflict.
2. Conduct postconflict discussions in person whenever possible to rebuild trust.
3. Remind the group that the aftermath might be uncomfortable, but it is an opportunity for the team to re-establish its commitment to each other and develop resiliency to handle the future disagreements that are inevitable in any collaboration.
4. Discuss how the group managed the conflict by balancing positives with negatives.
5. Schedule at least one session to discuss group lessons learned from the conflict.
6. Modify "ground rules" and group norms for disagreement, as needed.

Summary

To succeed, collaborators should be self-aware of their individual responses to conflict on three levels:

1. Emotional
2. Physiological
3. Cognitive

Emotional reactions can include fear, frustration, anger, impatience, uncertainty, resentment, and avoidance. Some examples of physiological reactions are rapid heart rate, sweating, increased adrenaline, tightening of one's vocal cords, nausea, and digestive issues, to name a few. For self-protection and also by force of habit, individuals typically respond to conflict in one of three ways: fight, flight, or passive-aggressive.

The cognitive responses to conflict involve views about conflict itself: levels of comfort or discomfort, and attitudes about the best way to handle it. Some cognitive responses are personal and cultural attitudes, values, and beliefs about conflict that contribute to one's overall mental perception of it.

There are two key strategies that are especially useful for navigating conflict in a collaboration, as follows:

- Setting expectations for interacting and communicating.
- Identifying the conflict stage and applying targeted strategies for that stage.

The first strategy, setting expectations for communicating, involves planning for how the parties will interact during times of tension, disagreement, and more emotionally charged conflicts. The second strategy is identifying the specific stage of the conflict, and then applying appropriate tactics to manage that stage efficiently.

The four stages of conflict include: Dormant, Emerging, Active, and Aftermath, and each one can be managed proactively with dedicated strategies. Among the strategies for managing the Dormant stage, the most important one is to remind all group members that expressing differing ideas is essential for a successful collaboration. During the Emerging stage, a key strategy is to remind each member that disagreement, when managed proactively, can foster increased innovation, so it is important to share any concerns before they escalate. When conflict is in the Active phase during a collaboration, an essential strategy is to encourage members to ask questions to understand motivations and not judge external behaviors as much. Finally, during the Aftermath stage, an important strategy is to conduct postconflict discussions with participants and witnesses to help identify lessons learned and rebuild trust.

CHAPTER 7

Collaborating for Innovation And Change

It is amazing what you can accomplish if you do not care who gets the credit.

—Harry S. Truman

Preview

This chapter highlights practical guidelines for attaining innovation and change most effectively by means of collaboration. The first step is to recognize that open communication between diverse thinking styles is necessary to generate the widest range of creative possibilities. The next approach is to ensure that the entire group, and not just one or two individuals, takes credit and accountability for the ideas generated. The third action is to allot enough time for unrestricted thinking. To achieve peak creativity, the collaboration team should focus first on generating ideas and options, and avoid talking too soon about implementation details such as budget, resources, and deadlines. This requires being willing to experiment, explore, risk failure, try again, test, and reinvent ideas freely without being distracted by practical considerations.

The fourth suggestion is to stretch one's imagination to its limits by combining an equal number of logical, factual, left-brain approaches, with more intuitive, right-brain methods. The final guideline is to encourage the group to employ a variety of visual, auditory, sensory, and tactical inputs to inspire diverse thinking styles to generate the widest range of ideas before narrowing down the options later in the process.

Five Guidelines for Generating Ideas

Collaboration is not just about communication; it is also a thinking process that the group does together with the intent to explore, discuss, invent, experiment, challenge, test, and refine ideas freely. Merging different perspectives in a collaboration takes tremendous mental effort and planning to comprehend how someone else could possibly conceive of an idea that can be totally different than one's own way of thinking. Although the collaboration journey is not always a smooth path, collaborators can achieve amazing results by exercising patience and diligence to explore and combine diverse ideas and perspectives.

Exploring and creating new approaches in a collaboration requires the team's collective commitment to be curious about each other's ideas, listen critically, ask engaging questions, and keep an open mind. There are five simple guidelines a collaboration team can implement to generate the most innovative concepts and options, as follows (Table 7.1):

Table 7.1 Idea generation guidelines

Collaboration is a Thinking Process				
1	2	3	4	5
Share accountability for creating new ideas as a group	Create a strong group connection of trust and commitment to innovation	Focus on generating ideas first before worrying about how to execute them	Use all of your brain: left + right = whole	Use diverse methods to explore possibilities through variation, not repetition

Guideline 1: Share Accountability for Creating Ideas

Since the true purpose of a team collaboration is to generate ideas one could not think of alone, it is paramount for all group members to accept that ownership is shared among everyone, and not just by one person. When a collaboration partner prefers to take all of the credit for ideas that were created by the team, this can erode trust, so egos need to be left behind. This is especially hard to do early in a collaboration when the parties are still building relationships. There could be a concern that someone will steal another's idea and take credit for it personally, when actually, each team member contributed in some way to the end result. As well, contractual or legal requirements could require restricting the ownership or copyright to only a few individuals in the group.

There are a few ways to manage the way the collaboration team creates and owns ideas:

1. Discuss and agree on definitions and guidelines for what shared ownership of cocreated ideas involves, so everyone is clear about what that commitment entails.
2. Consult a lawyer specializing in collaboration to make sure all aspects of shared idea ownership have been addressed. Make any necessary changes to the parameters or agreements that might affect patents, copyrights, and related applications.
3. Ask all team members to sign a nondisclosure agreement to ensure the confidentiality of information.
4. Include details about shared intellectual property ownership in the contractual agreements between the parties, and get legal advice before finalizing any of these documents.

Guideline 2: Create a Strong Group Connection

There are a few ways to facilitate group connections and help encourage commitment to sharing ownership for group ideas. These tactics include:

1. Strengthen the group's identity as cocreators by asking them to formulate a name, vision, motto, or goal for idea generation.
2. Discuss the benefits of shared group ownership of cocreated ideas.
3. Address concerns and laws regarding shared ownership of cocreated ideas, such as intellectual property and the use of social media.
4. Communicate clearly about the scope of what shared ownership includes and excludes, so there are no misunderstandings or potential legal issues.

Guideline 3: Focus on Ideas First

Freedom from restrictions on what or how to think is essential for effective idea generation in a collaboration. This means focusing more on the "what" of ideas, without getting sidetracked by the "how." To put practicalities such as budgets, deadlines, and resources on hold temporarily for the purpose of freeing one's mind to invent ideas is difficult for pragmatic and action-oriented individuals. The ambiguity of not knowing what to recommend or how to do it exactly might make one feel uncomfortable at first. Nonetheless, ambiguity is often needed to stimulate the most creativity.

It is difficult to restrain group members from closing out options and determining action steps too fast, especially if there are a few dominant personalities who want to influence others to do this. Nonetheless, there are a few proven tactics for how to keep the group focused on generating ideas first, without becoming distracted and losing focus:

1. Communicate and enforce clear "ground rules" to generate ideas only and avoid getting stuck in details.
2. Create a "Parking Lot" list of tactical details to address later, after the idea generation stage is completed.
3. Schedule dedicated days for idea generation, and assign other days for decision making, planning, execution, and evaluation.
4. Ensure that all ideas are acknowledged first without evaluation or judgment.
5. Generate a list of questions prior to each idea generation session to give all parties an opportunity to think ahead and be more prepared to contribute their best creative ideas.
6. Set milestones for generating creative ideas and celebrate each one as a group.
7. Invite visitors to join the group to share stories or methods for generating the best creative ideas.
8. Schedule idea generation meetings at peak energy hours to ensure maximum productivity.

Guideline 4: Use All of Your Brain: Whole-Brain = Left and Right Combined

Experienced collaborators know that exploring and inventing ideas is not a linear process. Ideas come and go from both the left and right sides of the brain. The left side is responsible for rational, objective, linear, deliberate, and logical sequencing. In contrast, the right side of the brain is nonlinear, intuitive, emotional, spontaneous, and inconsistent. The left part of the brain contributes by adding structure, analyzing details, providing a specific context, and reducing ambiguity in an orderly way. In contrast, the right part of the brain has more of a random, free-flowing approach that thrives on free association and ambiguity to generate as broad a range of options as possible.

Ultimately, combining left- and right-brain methods is the best approach to achieve peak creativity. It enables ideas based on rational thinking, research, facts, and data, while also imagining what-if scenarios, and using free association with words, pictures, people, products, places, and emotions. The whole-brain approach to idea generation in a collaboration is best described by this motto: "Plan but expect the unexpected; make lists but don't always use them; be rational but listen to your intuition as well; acquire facts and data, but don't rely on them; follow one's intuition but don't trust it fully."

There are many ways to blend left-brain and right-brain thinking for a whole-brain approach as follows:

- Enlist the support of the group to identify and discuss as many left-brain, fact-based questions, and right-brain, intuitive questions for maximum idea generation.
- Divide the group into two subteams, each one dedicated to generating left- or right-brain ideas.
- Start with the thinking style, either left or right brain, that the group considers to be most challenging, and agree to create as many ideas as possible in a designated time period.
- Apply a variety of brain-stimulating resources and approaches for idea generation: auditory, visual, kinesthetic, and tactile. Examples are indicated as follows:
  o Auditory: Previews, summaries, paraphrasing, questions, and reading aloud.
  o Visual: Colors, posters, whiteboards, blackboards, flip chart paper, digital materials, illustrations, charts, diagrams, and data.

o Sensory: Explore using a digital app, take frequent breaks, and simulate a new process.

o Tactile: Use of Post-It® notes, access to physical examples of layouts or constructed models, opportunities to touch, and experiment with samples.

- Identify the general brain type tendencies for each individual in the collaboration group:

  o Discuss each individual's self-awareness of his or her thinking style strengths and preferences.

  o Acquire resources about left, right, and whole-brain self-assessments and resources.

Guideline 5: Explore Possibilities Using Diverse Methods

The biggest mistake one can make in a collaboration when attempting to generate creative ideas is to become too set in the routine of using the same methods without utilizing a variety of approaches. For example, when a collaboration team decides to "brainstorm" ideas the same way they have done for every meeting in the past, this monotony can cause team members to lose their creative inspiration. The following methods can help stimulate the creative thinking of collaboration team members, with the flexibility to work well in a digital or nondigital format, in person, or virtually.

Crawford Slip

This group brain-writing method is designed to accumulate the greatest number of ideas in the briefest period of time. Invented by Dr. C.C. Crawford at the University of California in 1926, what makes Dr. Crawford's method remarkable is the fact that he designed it especially to use handwritten comments on strips of paper people would cut out themselves, decades before Post-It® notes were invented in 1968. Now, the Crawford Slip method can be used with actual Post-It® notes, or by using digital collaboration tools such as Post-It-Plus™, and other digital apps.

The Crawford Slip process has three safeguards that make it ideal when collaborating to brainstorm fresh ideas for innovation and change. First, it begins with a thoughtful question to stimulate group members to truly think creatively. Second, it engages groups to review and discuss diverse ideas in a nonthreatening way. Finally, it challenges the group to make decisions together about what ideas will be their priority to develop in the collaboration.

The Crawford Slip method always begins by asking a specific question that is broad enough to generate a variety of responses, yet specific enough not to be too vague. Some examples of suitable questions include:

- What issues and concerns keep senior leaders in our organizations up at night?
- What are the key challenges our public stakeholders face when seeking benefits and services?
- Why is it so difficult for our staff to keep each other informed globally about product and project changes?
- What changes need to be made to become more productive?

The question should be both read aloud and shown visually to all collaboration parties for shared understanding and easy reference. Then, each party should have access to a minimum of 10 separate Post-it®notes for writing down 10 different answers, a number that Dr. Crawford recommended for each person as the most efficient minimum number to generate the greatest quantity of group answers. Next, the notes are compiled in one visual area, and then sorted by category. Then, the group filters their idea preferences. Typically in rounds two and three, each party votes for top choices for each idea category. Finally, in round four, the group uses a systematic voting process to identify their final best choices as a collective unit. The options that were not chosen are kept together as archived items to consider for future discussions.

Opposite Thinking

Another effective way to generate innovative ideas is the Opposite Thinking method.

Jessica Cryer, Partner at CSPN (Customer Service Professionals Network), identifies Opposite Thinking as one of her personal favorites among collaborative ideation techniques. Jessica explains Opposite Thinking as follows:

> To stretch the horizon of possibilities, Opposite Thinking helps teams to challenge their assumptions and biases about a problem in order to ideate around non-obvious solutions. It's a simple process that begins with listing individually two to five assumptions about the problem or potential solution, writing them on the left side of a piece of paper, and then sharing these assumptions with the group. Then, individually, one selects an assumption and defines one or two opposite realities on the right side of the paper. Finally, the group discusses the realities and how they affect the problem, and then writes down potential solutions in a third column.[1]

SCAMPER

This idea generation method is based on an acronym originally conceived by advertising executive, Alex Faickney Osborn, in 1953. It was then developed further by Bob Eberle, educational specialist, in 1971. The SCAMPER method is a right-brain tool based on a series of letters that can be addressed either in sequence or in any order.[2]

To apply SCAMPER efficiently in a group collaboration, start with any letter and write down as many words, phrases, ideas, concepts, pictures, and emotions associated with it. Each of the seven letters represents a different aspect of inquiry. Although there are a few basic questions associated with each letter, more questions can be asked as long as they

---

[1] Cryer, Jessica, Partner at CSPN (Customer Service Professionals Network). 2019 (October 9, November 11). E-mail messages with author.
[2] Bob, E. 1996. *Scamper: Games for Imagination Development*, i-6. Waco Texas: Prufrock Press Inc.

have something to do with that letter. The letters and examples of questions for each are identified below:

S ubstitute:
- If replaced with something different, what could that be?
- What other ideas, resources, products, services, or processes can be introduced or used instead?

C ombine:
- What different kinds of products, services, and processes can be added?
- What can you add or combine for different or improved results?

A dapt or adjust:
- What can be adapted or changed?
- What ideas, ingredients, processes, products, or services can be used?

M odify or magnify:
- If you changed the shape, ingredients, order, size, or process, what would be different?
- What other shapes, forms, or versions can be created?
- When you look at the topic through lenses that make it larger or smaller, what do you see, and what would you change?

P ut to another use:
- How can you use this better or differently?
- What other uses can be applied to achieve better efficiency, accuracy, engagement, or quality?

E liminate:
- What can you leave out?
- What can you take away or stop doing?
- What can be made unnecessary that is not needed anymore?

R everse or rearrange:
- What order or sequence can be reversed?
- How can you rearrange the process, order, or approach?
- What can be organized differently for better results?

The SCAMPER brainstorming method is employed successfully by many organizations when collaborating to generate innovative ideas for the future. McDonald's is one of these organizations. Michael Michalko, author of *Thinkertoys: A Handbook of Creative Thinking Techniques*,[3] explains in this groundbreaking book how Ray Kroc, salesman and entrepreneur, applied SCAMPER to make many improvements to expand McDonald's products, services, and revenue, including:

- *Magnify*: Create the Big Mac.
- *Put to Other Uses*: Lease and develop sites, and then re-lease them to the franchisees.
- *Rearrange*: Restructure the architecture with golden arches on the roof.[4]

Mind Mapping

The Mind Mapping method was created in 1972 by educational consultant, memory and speed-reading expert, Tony Buzan. Buzan invented and perfected it based on the concept of radiant thinking from the brain. The Mind Mapping method replicates visually how the brain functions by relying on free association of ideas, concepts, words, pictures, and emotions.

Buzan based the physical appearance of mind mapping on how the mind naturally processes information and experiences, including the following characteristics:

- Colorful
- Associative
- Multidimensional
- Pictorial
- Imaginative
- Analytical

---

[3] Michalko, M. *Thinkertoys: A Handbook of Creative Thinking Techniques*, 2nd ed, 107–108. New York: Ten Speed Press.
[4] ibid pp. 76–78.

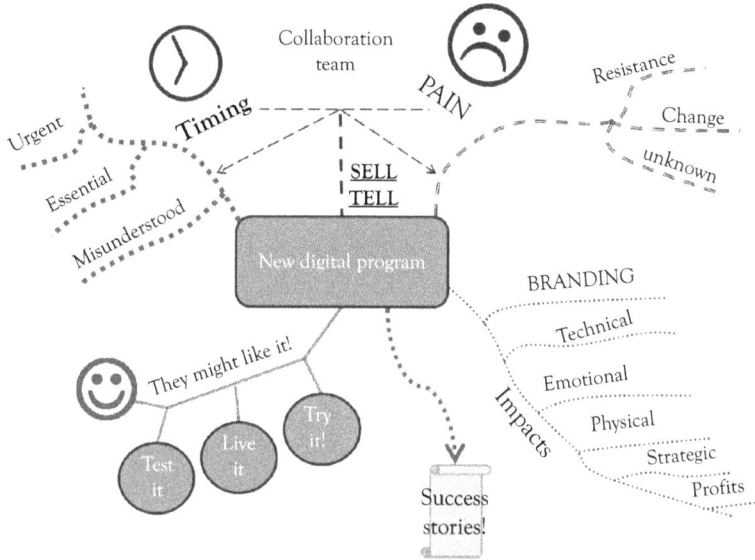

Figure 7.1 Mind mapping

- Verbal and nonverbal
- Not in any sequential order

Mind mapping (Figure 7.1) is an ideal method for collaborations because it is easy to execute, engages all types of thinking styles, and can be applied using simple resources such as markers and colored pencils, or more sophisticated digital apps. The following are some suggestions for how to create the best possible mind maps that leverage new ideas in a collaboration to the fullest extent possible:

1. Use a variety of many colors.
2. Do not restrict the shapes to circles or boxes.
3. Experiment by drawing images that stimulate the imagination more.
4. Think big: add emotions, taste, smell, and places.
5. Don't rely on just one mind map; create a series of mind maps that capture different associations to generate more ideas.
6. Make it fun: divide the group into smaller teams, and consider having a contest for the best one.
7. Take advantage of digital technology to experiment.

8. Go beyond the obvious: write down anything that comes to mind, even if it is not complete, and does not seem to connect logically.

9. Record whatever comes to mind, in any order.

Summary

Collaboration is not just about communication. It is also a thinking journey that the group takes together with the intent to explore, discuss, challenge, and refine ideas they cocreate collectively and could never invent by themselves. There are four simple guidelines to follow for achieving maximum creativity in a collaboration.

The first guideline is to share accountability for ideas that are cocreated by the group members. This includes getting buy-in and commitment at the beginning for the collective ownership of ideas, and getting legal advice about related issues, such as intellectual property, copyrights, and patents.

The second guideline is to focus on generating ideas first, before discussing practicalities. This involves avoiding any discussion about tactics and action steps until the maximum number of ideas have been generated.

The third guideline is to use a whole-brained approach by applying both left- and right-brain thinking. The best way to describe a whole-brain approach is this motto: "Plan but expect the unexpected; make lists but don't always use them; be rational but listen to your intuition as well; acquire facts and data, but don't trust it fully; follow one's intuition, but don't trust it fully."

The final guideline for generating the most creative ideas is to apply diverse approaches. Suggested methods for idea generation in collaborations include Crawford Slip, Opposite Thinking, SCAMPER, and Mind Mapping. The Crawford Slip is a systematic idea generation method with more of a left-brain than right-brain emphasis based on asking a key question and asking each person to contribute at least 10 answers to that question by writing them on individual Post-it® notes. Opposite Thinking involves identifying two to five assumptions about™ a problem, or potential solution, listing these assumptions on the left side of the paper, and then after group discussion, choosing one assumption to focus on and explore based on one or two opposite realities about it. This process enables individual reflection and group discussion about potential solutions that are listed in a third column.

SCAMPER is a right-brained, creative brainstorming method, based on answering questions related to each of seven changes for the future: substitute, combine, adapt or adjust, modify or magnify, put to another use, eliminate, and reverse or rearrange. Mind Mapping is also a right-brained method based on creating a visual representation of the human brain, using shapes, colors, concepts, words, and pictures to explore new ideas. It is ideal for creative idea generation because it is highly interactive, and participants can invent their own visual structures to replicate their thinking in unique ways.

CHAPTER 8

Overcoming Obstacles to Collaboration

The harder the conflict, the more glorious the triumph.

—Thomas Paine

Preview

Collaborating takes time, commitment, and effort to overcome the many obstacles along the way and achieve the best results. Successful collaborators need the resiliency and strategic know-how to overcome those obstacles proactively to attain the desired outcomes. This chapter identifies 10 common obstacles to collaboration as follows:

1. Unrealistic expectations about collaboration as a process.
2. Difficulty scheduling meetings that will be convenient for all parties to attend.
3. Lack of accountability to follow through on commitments.
4. Incompatible and dominant personalities.
5. Technology tools not integrated for everyone's access and ease of use.
6. Discomfort sharing knowledge and resources.
7. Lack of sponsorship from senior executive leaders.
8. Organizational bureaucracy restricting change initiatives.
9. Lack of diverse membership and representation.
10. Change of leadership during the collaboration.

Strategies for how to overcome each of these obstacles proactively are also provided.

Identifying 10 Collaboration Obstacles

Like any worthwhile process, collaboration is hard work, especially due to the inevitable challenges that occur. How collaborators handle these challenges can make a big difference regarding whether or not their collaboration efforts result in success or failure. Being well-prepared to address expected and unexpected obstacles proactively enables collaborators to become more resilient, productive, and effective.

The top 10 obstacles that collaborators are most likely to encounter include: unrealistic expectations, scheduling meetings for busy people, low accountability, dominant personalities, nonintegrated technology, poor knowledge transfer, inadequate sponsorship, organizational bureaucracy, lack of diverse membership, and changes in leadership. The following guidelines offer the secrets to success for overcoming these common collaboration challenges for optimal results (Table 8.1).

Unrealistic Expectations About Collaboration As a Process

The first obstacle to overcome is perhaps the most crucial one, namely unrealistic expectations about collaboration as a process. Some contributing factors include underestimating the amount of time required, wanting the collaboration to progress faster, and not expecting to need to invest

Table 8.1 Anticipating and overcoming obstacles

Obstacle #	Obstacle to Overcome
1	Unrealistic expectations about collaboration as a process
2	Difficulty scheduling meetings for all parties to attend
3	Lack of accountability to follow through on commitments
4	Incompatible and dominant personalities
5	Technology tools not used consistently by all parties
6	Not sharing knowledge and resources
7	Lack of sponsorship at the senior executive level
8	Organizational bureaucracy restricting change initiatives
9	Lack of diversity in the collaboration team
10	Change of leadership within the collaboration team

so much energy and patience to build trusting relationships. Expectations are hard to change, but addressing them in a timely manner is a good first step. Following are some strategies for how to uncover and manage unrealistic expectations proactively:

- Identify individual expectations: Ask each party to identify what he or she expects for the collaboration to be most effective:
  o Conduct a precollaboration survey or interviews to identify expectations.
  o Schedule a precollaboration meeting to reveal individual expectations of the team.
- Agree on expectations as a collaboration team:
  o Facilitate group discussion and agreement on what to expect, realistically, from the collaboration process.
  o Agree on which specific expectations are achievable, and which ones are not.
  o Agree on how to manage the collaboration process best, including roles and responsibilities for each party.
  o Offer those whose expectations are still not met, the option of withdrawing from the team and being replaced by another person.
- Identify key milestones and dates when the group will "check in" to discuss and evaluate progress.
- Invite a collaboration specialist to meet with the group to present information about what to expect realistically from collaboration as a process:
  o Offer advice to the group.
  o Agree to consult again about expectations, as needed.
- Cocreate new collaboration goals that are most achievable for the group:
  o Make the goals "SMART": specific, measurable, achievable, realistic, and time-bound.
  o Rank the goals based on the priority level for what is most important and achievable.
  o Identify unrealistic goals and eliminate them from the group's list.

Difficulty Scheduling Meetings That All Parties Can Attend

Scheduling a date and time when everyone is available to meet is another common obstacle to collaboration. Assuming that all parties have other commitments besides the collaboration, it is usually difficult finding a common date and time that is suitable for everyone. The more people involved in the collaboration, the more challenging it is to ensure optimal attendance that is convenient for everyone's schedule. The best strategies for managing this obstacle are as follows:

- *Assign backup representatives*: Request that each party choose one or two competent people as substitutes to represent them if needed.
- *Schedule multiple meetings in "clusters" ahead of time:* Use specialized software to poll all parties to identify a series of dates and times when all or most people are available and ask them to reserve these meetings well in advance.
- *Agree on the minimum number of attendees required to avoid cancelling meetings:* Enable the group to decide how many attendees need to attend for meetings to proceed as scheduled with a core group of people.
- *Determine scheduling procedures for changes and cancellations:* To avoid last-minute changes and cancellations, ask the group to agree on a reasonable time reframe to change or cancel meetings, and get everyone's commitment to comply.
- *Rotate meeting locations*: Schedule a variety of sites, combining both in-person and virtual meeting formats, to accommodate everyone.
- *Establish meeting time limits*: Shorter meetings will most likely appeal to all parties and result in optimal attendance.
- *Get agreement on the minimum number of meetings required to sustain membership:* Establish guidelines for the minimum number of meetings to attend or miss to be entitled to sustain one's membership on the collaboration team.

Lack of Accountability to Follow Through on Commitments

How can a collaboration team ensure that each individual follows through on promises to honor the commitments that are critical for success? The following are suggestions for how to motivate accountability:

- *Make it a privilege to join the collaboration team:* Communicate high standards of accountability to remain on the team, including completing assignments and actions on schedule and modeling the values and behaviors of a team charter that details accountabilities for each member.
- *Create a collaboration vision that all members support:* Team members are more likely to be accountable for tasks and projects they promise to deliver if they understand how these tasks and projects are aligned to the collaboration team's vision. This knowledge can motivate individual responsibility and accountability based on knowing how and why following through on one's promises affects both the team and the collaboration results.
- *Form an "Accountability Committee" to encourage and support participation:* An "Accountability Committee" is especially useful for complex collaborations with diverse members in multiple geographic locations representing different backgrounds and cultures. This committee can be a permanent core group, or a group that changes continuously, based on a rotating membership. The advantage of this committee is that it is created solely for the purpose of helping all collaboration parties achieve their commitments by providing advice, resources, ideas, and information.

Incompatible and Dominant Personalities

There are some effective ways to manage challenging personalities proactively in collaborations. The following strategies are recommended:

- *Appoint an experienced facilitator:* This person's role is to engage the group and manage dominant speakers at meetings with a balance of assertiveness and empathy.

- *Don't make it personal*: Talk to those individuals who are least and most dominant and encourage the quieter ones to speak more, and the more talkative ones to speak less.
- *Ask the group:* Get input for ideas about how they can achieve equal participation from all to hear everyone's views.
- *Assign roles at meetings:* Give dominant speakers roles that will still enable them to participate actively, such as taking notes, or to encourage others to speak.
- *Invite guest speakers:* Consider asking guest speakers specializing in personality and behavior styles to share their knowledge and provide coaching or mentoring to improve interpersonal communications within the team.

Technology Tools Not Used Consistently By All Parties

Despite continuous improvements in technology, collaboration teams still have difficulties ensuring that everyone can access the technology tools that will enable the collaboration team to communicate most efficiently. The following are suggestions for how to encourage all parties to use designated technology platforms, software, and apps consistently as a unit:

- *Keep it simple by choosing technology that is easy to use*: Use tools that are most likely to be compatible with all computer systems and software.
- *Make it essential:* Apply it to common tasks such as meeting agendas, updates, and information sharing.
- *Survey all parties to identify what technologies they use, prefer, and dislike*: This will help identify technology commonalities and gaps requiring improvement.
- *Assign an IT specialist to be on-call for troubleshooting issues:* Designate this person as a resource to all parties to assist with integration and system issues for all locations where the parties work or reside.
- *Test first before implementing:* Test technology and software options with members of the collaboration team before making any decisions about which ones to use or invest in.

- *Experiment with technology apps:* Encourage experimentation with new technology applications for meetings, updates, information sharing, and idea generation.
- *Ensure that the meeting location has maximum digital access:* Choose in-person and virtual meeting rooms that enable maximum access to technology. Avoid locations that are remote with limited or no wireless access.
- *Use technology carefully:* Communicate using technology to inform and influence with care. Avoid overusing e-mails and providing nonessential documentation to avoid creating unnecessary bureaucracy and eroding trust.

Not Sharing Knowledge and Resources

Another obstacle to a collaboration occurs when information, knowledge, and resources are withheld from the other parties, either due to discomfort or resulting from confidentiality requirements. Whereas in a competitive negotiation, withholding information might be considered a power play, in a collaborative negotiation, withholding information can damage relationships, since sharing information is a sign of trust in a partnership. To encourage information sharing and knowledge exchange between all collaboration parties, the following actions are recommended:

- *Set expectations for knowledge sharing:* Emphasize knowledge sharing as an essential team value expected throughout the collaboration process.
- *Assign subteams with differing but complementary knowledge and skills to work together:* This will enable more diverse perspectives by means of knowledge exchange to generate the most innovative options and solutions.
- *Select a meeting space most suitable for information exchange:* Choose to meet in a space with features that optimize interpersonal communications, including: good acoustics, flexible seating options, face-to-face visibility, and a quiet, isolated environment without any distractions.

- *Showcase individual knowledge and talent at group meetings*: Schedule regular mini-presentations and discussions to highlight individual expertise, encourage knowledge transfer, and build new skills within the team.
- Create an internal knowledge and resource-sharing website for team members only.

Lack of Sponsorship From the Senior Executive Level

A key factor in the success of any collaboration is endorsement from leaders and sponsors. This can involve support from a board of directors, a special committee of senior executives from all of the collaboration parties' organizations, or a volunteer group of people who have political clout. Senior-level sponsors can enforce considerable political and budgetary power to promote the great ideas that collaborations achieve. Otherwise, there is the risk that the collaborators will not be able to sell or execute their ideas effectively due to lack of political backing, limited budgets, and insufficient resources. Savvy collaborators can do much to acquire sponsorship for their projects and programs, including the following actions:

- *Promote sponsorship as a prestigious role:* Appoint one or more individuals from the collaboration team to identify the many benefits of sponsorship. Ensure that the short- and long-term interests of potential sponsors are identified clearly. If appropriate, seek the help of someone who has networking and sponsorship experience and a proven record of success.
- *Recruit senior-level sponsors at the beginning of the collaboration:* Identify the ideal potential partners for the collaboration. Approach these individuals to ask for their support and identify potential benefits for sponsorship.
- *Make the sponsors a part of the success story:* Engage the sponsors to tell the collaboration team's story to leverage political, educational, budgetary, and resource support. Involve the sponsors by asking for insights, expertise, and ideas to help build ownership for achieving the best collaboration outcomes.

Organizational Bureaucracy Restricting Change Initiatives

There is nothing more frustrating than creating innovative solutions that are delayed or eliminated due to bureaucratic obstacles and restrictions. When the organizational hierarchy overcomplicates policies and procedures, this hurdle can threaten the capacity of the collaboration team to attain internal approvals and initiate change in a timely manner. The following strategies can streamline processes and systems to minimize bureaucratic obstacles to change initiatives:

- *Determine what processes and policies are involved:* Identify the specific bureaucracies that can cause unnecessary restrictions or delays.
- *Identify specific improvements required for faster execution:* It is crucial to be able to identify exactly which bureaucracies are blocking the progress of the collaboration, and determine the changes necessary for increased efficiencies.
- *Get commitment from bureaucrats involved to help streamline processes:* The bureaucrats involved have the potential to improve processes to improve quality and efficiency. Their commitment can be acquired in the following ways:
  o *Appealing to their interests:* productivity, client or public satisfaction, and enhanced teamwork are a few examples.
  o *Asking for advice:* request that the bureaucrats advise how to simplify a complicated process or procedure to help make the necessary improvements.
  o *Conducting a test pilot:* seek support through calculated risk-taking to evaluate and refine ideas and changes before implementing the entire recommendation fully.
  o *Using referent power:* refer to the person, group, or organization that has the knowledge and authority to improve or override bureaucratic processes to enable the solutions to be implemented successfully.

Lack of Diverse Membership and Representation

The most successful collaborations result when different perspectives are combined into multiple options and solutions that one could never have created alone. A diverse membership based on different cultures, genders, ages, specializations, experiences, capabilities, and perspectives is like a breath of fresh air for any collaboration. This diversity of thinking fosters the broadest range of possible ideas to add energy and vitality to any collaboration to create the best possible discussions, options, and solutions. The following strategies enable collaborators to manage a lack of diverse membership and representation proactively:

- *Identify diversity gaps in the group:* Determine what constitutes "diversity" for the group and what gaps exist. Some of these categories include: mental capacity, physical capacity, age variation, and gender distribution.
- *Borrow it: Invite more diverse individuals to participate:* For example, if there is an opportunity to make the process of updating drivers' licenses more convenient, consider asking people that do not drive to provide their input. If there are no self-employed people on the collaboration team, consider inviting them to offer a different perspective.
- *Change it: Replace or add additional members as needed:* Sometimes it is better to replace or add additional members to a collaboration team to stimulate new ways of thinking.
- *Compensate for it: Ask for independent feedback*: Using interviews, surveys, or consultants, acquire input from additional individuals not represented in the core collaboration team to enable better idea generation, decision making, and problem solving.

Change of Leadership Within the Collaboration Team

It takes considerable time and effort for a collaboration team to achieve a high level of trust and peak performance together. Some of this comes from strong leadership within the team. Those sponsors and leaders who have a strong collaboration vision have the greatest potential to manage disagreement, idea generation, and decision making constructively. When these inspirational individuals leave a collaboration team, the team can experience uncertainty, loss and separation anxiety that can reduce their team synergy and cohesion significantly.

The following strategies are recommended when there is a change of leadership to help the team adjust faster to the leader's absence and continue to perform at their previous levels of trust and decision making:

- *Communicate the collaboration vision:* Unify the team by communicating the vision for the collaboration continuously and consistently. Introduce new leaders to the vision and remind the entire group that the vision is what unites the team in a common focus and purpose.
- *Form an orientation team:* By forming an internal orientation team to point out the cultural norms and working processes currently in place for the collaboration, members can help establish a seamless transition for new leaders who they rely on for collaboration support and success.
- *Appoint a mentor from within the team:* Allocating a team member to mentor any new leader(s) is a powerful way to advise them about current practices and consult on how and when to introduce any changes.

Summary

The 10 most common obstacles to a successful collaboration include: unrealistic expectations, scheduling conflicts, reduced accountability, dominant personalities, nonintegrated technology, poor knowledge transfer, inadequate sponsorship, organizational bureaucracy, lack of diverse membership, and adjustment issues due to changes in leadership. Key strategies for dealing with unrealistic expectations include identifying and addressing individual expectations, facilitating group agreement on what to expect realistically from the collaboration process, and cocreating new goals that are most achievable for the group. Regarding scheduling issues, two best practices are planning multiple meetings ahead of time so people can reserve dates, and establishing meeting time limits for peak engagement and to encourage maximum attendance.

To manage others' lack of accountability and commitment, strategies include: establishing high standards for team membership, creating a collaboration vision that the entire team supports, and forming an "Accountability Committee" to help members deliver on their promises by assisting with extra help or resources when needed. Strategies for dealing with incompatible or dominant personalities include assigning roles at meetings to give dominant speakers a break from speaking, and asking the group for ideas about how to ensure that all parties have the chance to voice their views equally.

Another obstacle, the lack of technology integration, can be addressed with these strategies: keeping it simple by choosing technology that is user-friendly, assigning an IT specialist to be available for troubleshooting problems, experimenting with efficient technology apps, and using technology carefully by minimizing the overuse of e-mails. Winning strategies for addressing a lack of sponsorship at the executive level involve: promoting sponsorship as an appealing activity, creating the demand for volunteers, recruiting senior sponsors at the very beginning of the collaboration, and making sponsors a part of the collaboration story by asking them to talk to others about small wins and successes.

Regarding organizational bureaucracy, strategies for making decision making and implementation more efficient include: determining what processes and policies need to be changed, identifying specific improvements for streamlining processes, and conducting a pilot test to take a calculated risk by executing solutions on a small scale first to evaluate and refine before launching them on a larger scale.

To increase diversity in the group, borrow it by inviting additional people with broader skills, interests, and experiences, change it by replacing or adding team members, and ask for independent feedback, using interviews, surveys, and consultants.

When there are leadership changes within the team, key strategies to overcome this upset are to remind everyone about the common vision for the collaboration, appoint a mentor from within the team to help new leaders adjust to the team culture, and implement changes gradually to enable members to adjust more easily.

Template 1

Self-Assessment of Collaboration Competencies

Name:

Date:

Purpose: To identify key collaborating strengths and areas for development.

Instructions: The following statements apply to 10 core competencies essential for collaboration success. These questions are grouped into a total of 10 category sections, each one representing a different collaboration competency. Identify how often you tend to think about and take action for each statement by rating the frequency based on this scale: 0 (never), 1 (rarely), 2 (sometimes), 3 (often), and 4 (always). To increase the accuracy of your responses, think about one or more specific collaborations you have been involved in, and answer the questions as honestly as possible.

To calculate your total score, add up the numbers in the Rating column. Each category of questions has a different scoring summary that interprets either higher or lower numbers as best, depending on the statements.

Answer Key for Category 1: Based on
Frequency

0 = I never think about it or do it

1 = I rarely think about it or do it

2 = I sometimes think about it or do it

3 = I often think about it or do it

4 = I always think about it or do it

1. Commitment: To take accountability by investing time and energy on an end goal

Template 1, Table 1.1 Commitment

	Questions	Rating 0–4
1.	I consider participating in collaborations to be a waste of time.	
2.	I prefer to spend more time on my tasks and deadlines than on collaborative decision-making about priorities.	
3.	I am willing to collaborate with others, even though I can get more done, and faster, by working on my own.	
4.	I have been told to collaborate, but if I had my own choice, I would not do it because it is not a priority for me right now, for various reasons.	
5.	I try to find ways to save time when collaborating so I can get back to my daily tasks and responsibilities.	
6.	I feel impatient in collaborations because they take too long.	
7.	I am doing everything I need to do to be a successful collaborator, so getting feedback on what I can change is not necessary.	
8.	I am collaborating only because my company considers it to be the popular new trend, like an ice cream "flavor of the month."	
9.	I just don't have the physical and mental energy required to withstand the pressures of a collaboration.	
10.	I am the only person in the collaboration who is truly accountable.	
	Total Commitment Score:	

Interpreting Your Commitment Score:

30 to 40 points: Your commitment to collaborating is at the lowest level, even though you probably have good reasons. You have the potential to be more effective as a collaborator once you are able to invest in the mindset, time and energy required for success.

20 to 29 points: Your commitment level to collaborating is inconsistent. You are making an effort, but probably for good reasons, you are not committing as much as you have the potential to do.

11 to 19 points: Your commitment level to collaborating is moderate. You are taking accountability by investing time and energy on an end goal, and this has led to your current success. Yet, you have the potential to increase your commitment even more.

0 to 10 points: Your commitment level to collaborating is at its peak. You are determined to invest the time and effort, despite the demands on your time and energy, and you have developed a strong collaborative mindset.

To increase your commitment level:

- Stay focused on the goal and do not get distracted by details.
- Consider ways to streamline and delegate your workload for other projects and tasks.
- Develop more patience for the collaboration process.
- Get coaching and mentoring on additional collaboration techniques.
- Network and build partnerships with other collaborators to support your efforts.

Answer Key for Category 2: Based on
Frequency
0 = I never think about it or do it
1 = I rarely think about it or do it
2 = I sometimes think about it or do it
3 = I often think about it or do it
4 = I always think about it or do it

2. Connection: To develop trust and community with the other parties:

Template 1, Table 1.2 Connection

	Questions	Rating 0–4
1.	I know that developing trust is a priority in a collaboration, so I schedule as much time as needed to strengthen relationships with the other parties.	
2.	I am able to communicate with other collaborators openly, even if I do not agree with their views.	
3.	I am able to observe and "read" other collaborators' responses nonjudgmentally.	
4.	I can be firm with other collaborators without losing their trust.	

5.	I have a "you and me against the problem" mentality without blaming that helps build strong partnerships with those I collaborate with.	
6.	Other collaborators can trust me to keep their opinions and emotions confidential at all times.	
7.	I work hard at building an open and tolerant community of collaborators where all can express their ideas freely without judgment or negative consequences.	
8.	I find it easy to listen to others without interrupting them, especially when I do not agree with what they are saying.	
9.	I work hard to help other collaborators feel welcome and included, even if it takes time away from my busy schedule.	
10.	I feel comfortable expressing my emotions and ideas to other collaborators, without fear of their judgment.	
	Total Connection Score:	

Interpreting Your Connection Score:

30 to 40 Points: Your connection with other collaborators is at its peak level. You are demonstrating the attitude and actions required to develop trust and community with the other collaboration parties.

20 to 29 Points: Your connection with other collaborators is effective. You demonstrate the mindset and actions necessary to build strong connections. However, you have the capability to enhance these connections even more.

11 to 19 Points: Your connection with other collaborators is inconsistent. You have the opportunity to make stronger connections by adjusting your mindset and schedule to dedicate more effort to develop trust and community with the other parties.

0 to 10 Points: Your connection with other collaborators is at its lowest level. You understand what is required but are not currently demonstrating the mindset and actions needed to develop trust and community with the other parties. When you decide that you are able to do this, you have the potential to develop open and trusting connections with other collaboration parties.

To increase your connections:

- Identify ways to streamline your schedule so you have more time to spend developing relationships with other collaborators.
- Ask successful collaborators to share tips on how to build stronger connections efficiently.
- Develop skills in asserting your ideas with more confidence and competence.
- Participate in networking and relationship-building activities to enhance your connection skills.
- Ask for feedback from others you trust for how to build strong connections based on your unique personality and strengths, and listen actively to what they tell you.

Answer Key for Category 3: Based on
Frequency
0 = I never think about it or do it
1 = I rarely think about it or do it
2 = I sometimes think about it or do it
3 = I often think about it or do it
4 = I always think about it or do it

3. Curiosity: To explore new ideas and approaches outside one's own views

Template 1, Table 1.3 Curiosity

	Questions	Rating 0–4
1.	I enjoy learning more about how others think, operate, work, and communicate, even if I do not agree.	
2.	I find it easy to concentrate on exploring new ideas and approaches despite the responsibilities of my own schedule and to-do list.	
3.	I prefer to hear others' views first before I tell them mine.	
4.	I like to ask collaborators lots of questions to understand their opinions without needing to agree or disagree with them.	

5.	I consider it very important in a collaboration to listen to as many perspectives as possible, regardless of how much time it takes.	
6.	I am able to concentrate on listening to others' views without getting distracted by my own thoughts.	
7.	I am comfortable with ambiguity and not knowing all the answers.	
8.	I make an effort to understand what people are trying to say, and encourage them to share their views, even if I do not agree.	
9.	I encourage people to explain their interests and concerns fully to me first, before I will challenge them or disagree.	
10.	I like to take risks based on trial and error, instead of always knowing what the end result will be.	
	Total Curiosity Score:	

Interpreting Your Curiosity Score:

30 to 40 Points: You demonstrate a high degree of curiosity that enables you to collaborate effectively to explore the unknown, accept ambiguity, and consider new ideas beyond your own knowledge and experience.

20 to 29 Points: Your curiosity is consistent when you collaborate. It enables you to encourage and listen to the views of other collaborators with interest, patience, and an open mind. You have the potential to increase your curiosity even more in collaborations to bring out the best ideas in others.

11 to 19 Points: You have curiosity as a collaborator, but you demonstrate it inconsistently. You have the opportunity to improve your curiosity by encouraging others more to communicate differing views, options, and solutions.

0 to 10 Points: Your curiosity as a collaborator is low. You understand what is needed and required, so you have the opportunity to improve and demonstrate more curiosity in collaborations with more practice.

To increase your curiosity:

- Develop more patience to listen to people explain their views, even if they do not communicate the same way as you.

- Prepare questions in advance that encourage others to share differing and opposing views.
- Create "ground rules" to build an open and accepting team climate that encourages idea exchange and knowledge.
- Get advice from skilled collaborators on how to deal with the unknown and become more comfortable with ambiguity.
- Take notes during collaborations: write down interesting ideas and options without needing to agree or act on them.

Answer Key for Category 4: Based on Frequency
0 = I never think about it or do it
1 = I rarely think about it or do it
2 = I sometimes think about it or do it
3 = I often think about it or do it
4 = I always think about it or do it

4. Convincing skills: To influence buy-in and manage disagreement proactively

Template 1, Table 1.4 Convincing skills

	Questions	Rating 0–4
1.	I am not comfortable influencing others with more authority than me when I collaborate.	
2.	I do not have any formal training in the persuasion process and how to apply it when collaborating.	
3.	In collaboration meetings, I prefer not to speak publicly when I do not know ahead of time exactly what to say.	
4.	I am not comfortable "thinking on my feet" without a lot of preparation time.	
5.	I do not have a mastery of influencing techniques for buy-in and commitment at all levels when collaborating.	
6.	I am not comfortable experiencing or watching disagreements in collaborations.	
7.	I am not comfortable disagreeing with others if I do not have time to review all the facts and data ahead of time.	
8.	I am not comfortable "selling" ideas to others in group settings.	
9.	In collaboration meetings with others present, I do not like to be asked questions I do not know the answers to.	

10.	I am not comfortable trying to influence people who challenge or criticize my views.	
	Total Convincing Score:	

Interpreting Your Convincing Score:

30 to 40 Points: Your convincing skills are at the lowest level of development. You understand what is needed, but you require more confidence and practice applying those skills when collaborating.

20 to 29 Points: Your convincing skills are inconsistent and have the potential to be applied more frequently. You know you require more effort and practice to enhance your convincing skills when collaborating.

11 to 19 Points: You are demonstrating convincing skills often and consistently when you collaborate. But you still have potential to develop your confidence and capabilities to be even more persuasive when collaborating.

0 to 10 Points: You are demonstrating convincing skills at a peak level when collaborating. You have the confidence and competence to persuade others consistently to achieve the desired collaboration outcomes.

To improve your convincing skills:

- Practice thinking on your feet without preparing in advance exactly what words you are going to say.
- Ask for feedback from others for how you can improve how you influence.
- Get coaching and mentoring from others who are successful influencing with and without authority.
- Enroll in courses on negotiating, persuading, and influencing; listen to podcasts; read books; and watch simulations on relevant strategies and tactics.
- Arrange for a negotiating or persuasion expert to tape you practicing a simulated convincing segment in a collaboration, review it with you, and then provide constructive feedback on how to improve.

Answer Key for Category 5: Based on
Frequency
0 = I never think about it or do it
1 = I rarely think about it or do it
2 = I sometimes think about it or do it
3 = I often think about it or do it
4 = I always think about it or do it

5. Communication agility: To convey constructive messages fluently and skillfully

Template 1, Table 1.5 Communication agility

	Questions	Rating 0–4
1.	I like being challenged in the moment to adapt my messages spontaneously to engage diverse people.	
2.	I seek opportunities to learn and practice new communication techniques, even though I do not know ahead of time how the other parties will respond.	
3.	I enjoy delivering messages in different ways to diverse groups of people.	
4.	I have technical training and practice revising, or "reframing" messages to inform and engage others.	
5.	I am quick to edit and refine messages to others in the moment with confidence and flexibility.	
6.	I prefer to adjust my communication style to my audience for maximum impact.	
7.	I deliver messages with a constructive intent that is hard on the problem and does not blame the person.	
8.	I acknowledge questions first before I respond to them.	
9.	I am both assertive and diplomatic when I communicate to others.	
10.	I respond to criticism nondefensively with poise and diplomacy.	
	Total Communication Agility Score:	

Interpreting Your Communication Agility Score:

30 to 40 Points: Your communication agility is at its peak. You are communicating constructive messages fluently and skillfully when you collaborate.

20 to 29 Points: You are demonstrating communication agility consistently when you collaborate. You have the potential to become even more skillful and fluent when you communicate.

11 to 19 Points: You demonstrate communication agility inconsistently when you collaborate. You understand what is required and can increase your communication agility with more effort and practice.

0 to 10 Points: Your communication agility is underdeveloped. You understand what is needed, and with effort and discipline, you have the opportunity to improve your communication agility.

To improve your communication agility:

- Practice responding to unexpected questions when you are not prepared with the answers.
- Ask for constructive feedback for how to adapt better to others' styles.
- Take risks by trying new communication approaches and asking for input.
- Learn and practice new techniques for communicating messages to people with diverse styles.
- Volunteer to participate in meetings and other events when you have the opportunity to explain or defend your views to people who challenge you.

Answer Key for Category 6: Based on
Frequency
0 = I never think about it or do it
1 = I rarely think about it or do it
2 = I sometimes think about it or do it
3 = I often think about it or do it
4 = I always think about it or do it

6. Cultural adaptability: To observe and adjust well to diverse values, beliefs, and norms

Template 1, Table 1.6 Cultural adaptability

	Questions	Rating 0–4
1.	I am knowledgeable about different cultures and how to adapt.	
2.	I observe others' time styles and make the best adjustments to adapt with cultural awareness and sensitivity.	
3.	I am self-aware of how my own cultural attitudes and beliefs can both help and hinder my collaboration effectiveness.	
4.	I consider cultural differences of both monochronic, linear time and polychronic, spontaneous time when I organize meetings and agendas for collaborations.	
5.	I do not make assumptions about how people think and do things, preferring instead to observe, ask questions, and adapt to each situation.	
6.	I ask nonjudgmental questions to learn more about the cultural values and practices of the people I collaborate with.	
7.	I do not make any assumptions or judgments about the cultures represented by the people I collaborate with.	
8.	I always ask for feedback regarding my cultural adaptability and how I can improve.	
9.	I make a conscious effort to adapt the content and format of collaborations to different cultures for maximum communications impact.	
10.	I avoid stereotyping or making insensitive comments and behaviors when collaborating to respect and adapt to collaborators from diverse cultures.	
	Total Cultural Adaptability Score:	

Interpreting your cultural adaptability score:

30 to 40 Points: Your cultural adaptability when collaborating with others has reached a peak level of awareness and effectiveness.

20 to 29 Points: When collaborating, you think about cultural adaptability often and usually consistently. You have the knowledge and confidence to enhance your ability to be even more culturally adaptable when you collaborate.

11 to 19 Points: Your cultural adaptability in collaborations is inconsistent. You know what you need to observe and do to adapt to other's values and beliefs to become more effective.

0 to 10 Points: Your cultural adaptability when collaborating is underdeveloped. You understand what is needed to increase your effectiveness. You have the opportunity to improve with more consistent effort and practice.

To improve your cultural adaptability:

- Learn more about cultural values and attitudes toward: time, space, technology, rules, gender, decision making, conflict, negotiating, and collaborating as a process.
- Ask for constructive feedback for continuous improvement.
- Seek input from cultural communication experts about how to improve your cultural adaptability.
- Ask collaborators with multicultural experience for advice about how to adapt your approach to engage diverse cultures.
- Participate in multicultural training for negotiations and collaborations.

Answer Key for Category 7: Based on
Frequency
0 = I never think about it or do it
1 = I rarely think about it or do it
2 = I sometimes think about it or do it
3 = I often think about it or do it
4 = I always think about it or do it

7. Courage: To take risks beyond one's own comfort zone to try new approaches

Template 1, Table 1.7 Courage

	Questions	Rating 0–4
1.	I have difficulty taking risks when collaborating because I fear the negative consequences.	
2.	I am most comfortable using the same processes and approaches when I collaborate because they always work well for me.	
3.	I do not see any reason to change and take risks beyond my comfort zone, since my approach to collaboration works fine as it is.	

4.	I do not like others to disapprove of what I say or do, so I am very cautious about saying or doing anything different or new that can be criticized.	
5.	I do not like uncertainty or not knowing what the results will be when I collaborate.	
6.	I prefer to make suggestions based on facts and proven evidence to reduce risks when I collaborate.	
7.	I am suspicious of others' suggestions if they are based on intuition, because facts are always best.	
8.	I am not comfortable communicating unpopular ideas or suggestions to others in collaborations.	
9.	I am not willing to go beyond my comfort zone to try new approaches because I have tried that before, and it did not work.	
10.	I prefer to know ahead of time when I collaborate what the results will be before I will recommend or agree to anything.	
	Total Courage Score:	

Interpreting your courage score:

30 to 40 Points: Your score shows that you have an underdeveloped capacity to take risks beyond your own comfort zone when you collaborate. You should try new approaches that showcase your courage more frequently the next time you collaborate.

20 to 29 Points: Your score indicates that you have an inconsistent approach to trying new approaches and taking risks beyond your own comfort zone. You understand what is required, though, and have the potential to take more risks more often in future collaborations to demonstrate courage more consistently.

11 to 19 Points: Your score shows that you are consistent in taking risks beyond your comfort zone to try new approaches when you collaborate. You have the potential to improve this competency even more in future collaborations.

0 to 10 Points: Your score reveals that you demonstrate courage at the highest level when you collaborate, by going beyond your comfort zone and trying new approaches, despite the risks.

To improve your courage when collaborating:

- Experiment with different processes and approaches without worrying about mistakes.
- Focus on lessons learned as more important than success or failure.
- Become more self-aware of your risk averse tendencies to gain more confidence.
- Trust your "inner voice" and try new approaches based on your intuition.
- Seek feedback when you take risks and adjust your approach each time.

Answer Key for Category 8: Based on Frequency
0 = I never think about it or do it
1 = I rarely think about it or do it
2 = I sometimes think about it or do it
3 = I often think about it or do it
4 = I always think about it or do it

8. Creativity: To apply both intuitive (divergent) and logical (convergent) brainpower

Template 1, Table 1.8 Creativity

	Questions	Rating 0–4
1.	I prefer to know the correct answers to questions ahead of time.	
2.	I do not like brainstorming when collaborating, since it is a waste of energy and nothing gets done.	
3.	I do not think it makes sense to explore ideas in a collaboration, if we do not have the resources, budget, and time to implement them effectively.	
4.	I do not feel comfortable spending time generating new ideas in a collaboration if what we are already doing works just fine.	
5.	I do not like spending time in a collaboration discussing vague or ambiguous ideas that are not clear or supported by facts.	
6.	I prefer to use a logical, linear process when generating new ideas during collaborations.	

7.	I do not like to use free-association and intuition to generate ideas in a collaboration because they are a waste of time.	
8.	I do not have any training in whole-brain thinking combining left- and right-brained techniques to use in collaborations.	
9.	I do not have any interest in learning or using whole-brain thinking techniques when collaborating.	
10.	I prefer to narrow down options quickly in collaborations to be more specific about what to do and how to do it.	
	Total Creativity Score:	

Interpreting your creativity score:

30 to 40 Points: Your creativity during collaborations is underdeveloped. You understand what is needed and you have the opportunity to be more creative more often, if you choose to make more of an effort.

20 to 29 Points: Your creativity during collaborations is inconsistent. You know what you need to do to be more creative. With continued effort, you can apply creative thinking more deliberately and frequently when you collaborate.

11 to 19 Points: You demonstrate creativity consistently during collaborations. You understand how to apply it already, and with more effort and practice, you have the potential to be even more creative when you collaborate.

0 to 10 Points: You demonstrate peak creativity when you collaborate. You make deliberate attempts in collaborations to apply a whole-brain approach to develop and expand on new ideas and options for optimal innovation and change.

To improve your creativity when collaborating:

- Be deliberate about choosing both linear, left-brain and more intuitive, right-brain approaches to generating ideas when collaborating.
- Develop your whole-brain thinking skills through reading, coaching, and training.
- Become self-aware of your own thinking style and how it can both help and hinder collaboration effectiveness for you and others.

- Learn to enjoy ideas in the moment, and not look for solutions too fast.
- Ask others, with different thinking styles, to suggest new ways to be creative when collaborating to generate ideas and make decisions.

Answer Key for Category 9: Based on
Frequency
0 = I never think about it or do it
1 = I rarely think about it or do it
2 = I sometimes think about it or do it
3 = I often think about it or do it
4 = I always think about it or do it

9. Conflict resolution: To manage disagreements confidently using proven strategies and tactics

Template 1, Table 1.9 - Conflict resolution

	Questions	Rating 0–4
1.	I do not feel comfortable with conflict during collaborations.	
2.	I prefer to ask someone else to manage disagreements during a collaboration so I won't be blamed.	
3.	I do not see the benefit of focusing on what "triggers" my conflict reactions when I experience tension, disagreements, or strong conflicts when collaborating.	
4.	I try to avoid conflict and disagreements as much as possible when I collaborate with others.	
5.	I am cautious and lack confidence managing conflict in collaborations because the situation can get worse very quickly.	
6.	I like to get my way when collaborating, especially when I know I am right.	
7.	I have not had any conflict management coaching or training.	
8.	I am not interested in applying conflict management techniques when I collaborate, because I have good instincts and common sense.	
9.	I prefer to encourage agreement during collaborations.	
10.	I don't think arguing is worth the energy, so I avoid disagreeing.	
	Total Conflict Resolution Score:	

Interpreting your conflict resolution score:

30 to 40 Points: Your conflict resolution competency as a collaborator is underdeveloped. You know it is important to manage conflict proactively, so with continued effort and training, you have the opportunity to apply conflict management more frequently when you collaborate.

20 to 29 Points: Your conflict resolution competency as a collaborator is inconsistent. You know what you need to do to address conflict with more confidence in collaborations. You have the potential to apply conflict management processes and techniques more consistently when you collaborate in the future.

11 to 19 Points: You manage conflict consistently in collaborations by using proven strategies and tactics with confidence. You are very self-aware of your conflict "triggers" and what you need to do more often to address and resolve conflicts in future collaborations.

0 to 10 Points: Your conflict resolution confidence and competence when collaborating is at a peak level. You are self-aware of your own "trigger" responses to conflict. You recognize that disagreement is crucial to the success of a collaboration, and take quick action to manage disagreement for effective conflict resolution.

To improve your conflict resolution skills when collaborating:

- Become more self-aware of what "triggers" your conflict responses.
- Recognize that disagreement is a natural and essential part of successful collaborations.
- Learn and practice conflict management techniques when collaborating.
- Get coaching on how you can manage conflicts better in collaborations.
- Get feedback from other collaborators on how you handle conflict individually and in group settings, and constructive ways to improve.

Answer Key for Category 10: Based on
Frequency
0 = I never think about it or do it
1 = I rarely think about it or do it
2 = I sometimes think about it or do it
3 = I often think about it or do it
4 = I always think about it or do it

10. Compliance: To construct and enforce consistent collaboration processes and protocols for success

Template 1, Table 1.10 Compliance

	Questions	Rating 0–4
1.	I prefer collaborations that are informal.	
2.	I prefer more of a spontaneous approach to collaboration without the formality of any structure.	
3.	I have a hard time convincing others to follow protocols and guidelines when collaborating.	
4.	I tend to overlook administrative tasks involved in collaborations because I am not detailed.	
5.	I do not have any training in group processes to implement when I collaborate.	
6.	I do not think that collaboration teams need a structured process for decision making; it is better just to figure it out less formally.	
7.	I avoid formal processes and administrative tasks in collaborations whenever possible because I do not like bureaucracy.	
8.	I am not comfortable about enforcing consistent group processes and protocols for collaborations.	
	Total Compliance Score:	

Interpreting your compliance score:

25 to 32 Points: Your interest in creating and enforcing consistent group processes and protocols when you collaborate is underdeveloped. You have the opportunity to recognize that the collaboration team can be more connected and productive by implementing structured procedures and processes for group discussion and decision making.

16 to 24 Points: You are initiating and encouraging group compliance to collaboration processes and protocols, but you need to do this more deliberately and consistently. You have the potential to formalize how you and others interact in collaborations for improved discussion and decision making.

9 to 16 Points: You are consistent in the amount of time and effort you spend constructing and enforcing consistent group processes when collaborating. You have the potential to initiate and implement group processes more often to help make the collaboration most efficient and effective.

0 to 8 Points: Your competency constructing and enforcing consistent group processes and procedures for effective collaborations is at a peak level. You are self-aware of your own attitudes about formalizing policies and procedures, and you are well versed in applying various techniques and approaches consistently to bring out the best in yourself and others when collaborating.

To improve your compliance skills when collaborating:

- Recognize that structured processes and protocols are not bad, and actually help make group discussions, debates, and decision-making more efficient and effective.
- Insist on using "ground rules" to establish group operating norms for the collaboration process.
- Learn new techniques for creating and enforcing more structured and formalized group processes for group discussion, debate, and decision-making.
- Learn and apply project management processes for planning, organizing, executing, and evaluating collaborations and related projects and programs.
- Interview successful collaboration facilitators and leaders for advice about how to motivate others to comply with collaboration processes and standards that contribute to better results.

Action Plan: Developing Your Collaboration Competencies

1. Identify one collaboration competency that you intend to work on developing more:

   • Competency: _____
   • One action step: What, with whom, how, when?

2. Identify one collaboration competency that you will continue developing as a collaborating strength:

   • Competency:_____
   • One action step: What, with whom, how, when?

Template 2

Planning Checklist for "Collaboration Mindfulness"

Name:

Date:

Purpose: To provide guidelines for how to achieve "collaboration mindfulness" for peak performance prior to each collaboration. The purpose of this checklist is to help you take a more deliberate and balanced approach to collaborating so you can become more focused, calm, assertive, and diplomatic. These guidelines can also be adapted for use as collaboration team "ground rules" for building trust and conducting constructive discussions.

Instructions:

- Read each of the following statements.
- Consider your own experiences and also input from others.
- Answer each statement as honestly as possible.

Questions (please circle your answers):

1. Are you convinced that a collaboration is the best process to use for achieving the results you want? Yes/No
2. Are you willing to consider alternative ideas and approaches that you would not typically think of, consider, or agree to, without others' input? Yes/No
3. Are you willing to dedicate the time and effort necessary to develop a trusting and unified partnership with the other collaborators? Yes/No

4. Are you able to converse and disagree with other collaborators without the mental interference of being defensive or territorial in your thinking? Yes/No

5. Are you willing to take all the time you need without rushing? Yes/No

6. Can you stay focused on the collaboration goal without getting distracted by unnecessary details and tangents? Yes/No

7. Can you ensure spending sufficient time to explore all possibilities before finalizing action steps? Yes/No

8. Can you accept that your way of thinking and doing things is not necessarily the only way, the right way, or the best way? Yes/No

9. Is your thinking focused on "we" instead of "me" to encourage shared ownership of ideas? Yes/No

10. Are you able to accept the ambiguity of not knowing all of the answers? Yes/No

11. Are you confident asking questions to enhance your understanding of what others say, even if you do not agree with them? Yes/No

12. Do you view all collaboration partners as having equally important status and titles? Yes/No

13. Is your mind focused on making changes for the future, instead of spending too much time thinking about the past? Yes/ No

14. Do you self-manage negative "triggers" effectively by relaxing mentally and physically? Yes/No

15. Do you work on accepting your strengths and limitations first, to make it easier for you to be more tolerant about the limitations as well as the strengths of others? Yes/No

16. Do you treat the other collaboration parties with empathy? Yes/No

17. Are you willing and able to accept disagreement nondefensively so you can truly listen and learn from others? Yes/No

18. Do you listen to understand, without needing to agree? Yes/No

19. Do you have the self-confidence to convey your ideas assertively? Yes/No

20. Are you able to communicate sensitive messages with honesty and tact? Yes/No

21. Are you willing to encourage others to convey their ideas assertively? Yes/No

22. Are you disciplined in following a systematic communication process in the collaboration for discussion, disagreement, and decision making? Yes/No

23. Are you able to remain curious about others' perspectives? Yes/No

24. Are you more focused on learning and growing through interactions and input from others, than on wanting to win? Yes/No

Scoring Instructions:

1. Add up the number of separate "yes" and "no" answers.

2. Use the following rating chart to assess the frequency of your "collaboration mindfulness":

How Many "Yes" Answers?	General Interpretation Guidelines
20 to 24	Demonstrates "Collaboration Mindfulness" Consistently
15 to 19	Demonstrates "Collaboration Mindfulness" Usually
10 to 14	Demonstrates "Collaboration Mindfulness" Sometimes
5 to 9	Demonstrates "Collaboration Mindfulness" Occasionally
0 to 4	Demonstrates "Collaboration Mindfulness" Rarely

3. Identify those answers you checked off as "yes" and choose one that you will continue to develop as a "collaboration mindfulness" strength.

4. Select one "no" answer that you will focus on developing more to develop your "collaboration mindfulness."

Template 3

Collaboration Process Planner

Name:
Date:
Collaboration Topic:
Collaboration Parties:
Purpose: To plan the collaboration process systematically by identifying key questions for individuals and teams to answer to prepare for a successful collaboration.

Discovery: Collaboration Purpose, People, and Perceptions

1. Why should there be a collaboration? What is the purpose?
2. What contribution will the collaboration accomplish?
3. What does "success" look like when the collaboration ends?
4. What do you know and understand about the motivations, expertise, values, and concerns of the collaboration parties?
5. What is the collaboration vision for the team?
6. What are the core values for the team?
7. What are the key roles and responsibilities for the team?
8. What scheduling process will be used to ensure maximum attendance at meetings?
9. Where will meetings take place?
10. How will collaboration team members keep each other informed and updated?
11. What does each person need from the others for support during the collaboration?
12. What makes this collaboration unique?
13. What will the collaboration achieve that is innovative?

Discussion: Give and Take Input and Suggestions

1. What are the key topics and issues that need to be addressed?
2. What is the key goal for the collaboration?
3. How will group discussions be structured?
4. How will time be managed most effectively?
5. What communication media will be used, including meeting minutes and other documentation and digital media, to plan, organize, and debrief for discussions?
6. How will scheduling and other administrative logistics be managed to make the collaboration most efficient?
7. What are key problems and concerns to be addressed in the collaboration?
8. What are key opportunities to be addressed in the collaboration?
9. What are the acceptable behaviors for collaboration team members at meetings?
10. What are the "ground rules" for managing collaboration discussions most effectively?
11. What methods will be used to encourage the open exchange of information among diverse parties during the collaboration?

Disagreement: Address Objections and Differences Proactively

1. Why is disagreement crucial for the collaboration team to succeed?
2. How can the team encourage and manage disagreement during discussions to encourage differing viewpoints without judgment?
3. How can the team encourage maximum participation during disagreements?
4. How will the team manage conflict proactively?
5. What are the team "ground rules" for how to disagree appropriately?
6. How will the team address negative behaviors during the collaboration?

Agreement: Finalize Decisions, Contracts, Ownership, Responsibilities, and Actions

1. What decision-making methods will be put into practice?
2. What is the group process for how decisions will be challenged and agreed to?
3. What processes will be used to make sure decisions are not made too soon or delayed too long?
4. How will decisions and related action plans be documented, monitored, updated, and archived?
5. Who will "own" the ideas and decisions made, including proprietary ownership of intellectual property?
6. What does each collaboration team member need to do to demonstrate accountability for decisions made and actions to be taken?
7. Who will finalize and administer contracts, patents, and other legal agreements?

Template 4

Problem and Opportunity
Topic Planner

Date:

Name:

Purpose: To ensure the best possible outcomes by determining first the best topic focus for the collaboration: problem or opportunity focus? Instructions: Complete the following template and answer the key questions to help you determine the topic focus of the collaboration.

Template 4, Table 4.1 Problem Versus Opportunity

Template:

- What is the general topic for the collaboration?

  _____

- Describe the topic from both perspectives: problem and opportunity:

Template 4, Table 4.2 Problem and Opportunity

Problem As Is: present state	Opportunity Can Be: future state
Describe the present problem: what needs to be addressed for the present?	Describe the future opportunity: what can be changed for the future?

List related issues and questions:	List related issues and questions:
What needs to be resolved?	What needs to change?
Reword the "problem" (concise question or statement)	Reword the "opportunity" (concise question or statement)

Key Questions to Explore

Problem:

1. What is the apparent problem?
2. Is your answer to question 1 actually the problem, or is it the symptom of a root cause?
3. What is the context of the problem: background, assumptions, causes, and pertinent details?
4. What is the supporting data and research?
5. What has been done in the past to resolve the same or similar problems?
6. What systems, policies, and procedures are currently involved?
7. How effective are these?
8. What specific actions need to take place to resolve the problem?
9. What are some innovative solutions to consider?
10. What are the requested or required timelines?
11. How will the results be measured?
12. Is a collaboration the best way to resolve the problem?

Opportunity:

1. What is the perceived opportunity?
2. What are other related opportunities?
3. What is the actual opportunity that is best to focus on?
4. What are the benefits of pursuing the opportunity?
5. What are the risks if the opportunity is not pursued?
6. What are some current ideas that can be adapted to develop the opportunity?
7. What are some innovations and trends that should be considered?
8. What data and research supports pursuing this opportunity?
9. What are some new ideas that can be invented as a result of the opportunity?
10. What would motivate you as a stakeholder about this opportunity?
11. What would demotivate you as a stakeholder about this opportunity?
12. What would motivate the intended target group(s) or end user(s) about this opportunity?
13. What would demotivate the intended target group(s) or end user(s) about this opportunity?
14. Is a collaboration the best way to address the opportunity?

Template 5

Negotiating and Influencing Tip Sheet

Name:

Date:

Purpose: To acquire useful tips and relevant techniques for more effective negotiating and influencing in a collaboration.

Tip #1: Use a variety of question types to attain a complete understanding of the other parties.

Types of Questions and Examples:

1. **Reality Check:** What is your understanding of the problem?
2. **Hypothetical:** Suppose you are the taxpayer. What would be your concerns?
3. **Emotional thermometer:** How confident do you feel about this being the right decision?
4. **Implications:** How do you think the accounting staff will be affected by this change?
5. **Trial balloon:** Would you consider conducting a test program, assuming we can agree on the budget today?
6. **Leading:** Based on your questions, have you considered that this might not be the best time to implement the program?
7. **Suppose:** Supposing we invent a new way to track customer inquiries, what new information do you think we would want to learn?
8. **Open-ended:** What ideas do you have?
9. **Closed-ended:** Do you agree with that recommendation?
10. **Rhetorical:** Are we a brilliant collaboration team, or what? So what else can we think of doing that is brilliant?

11. **Trigger:** How can you be certain that the Board will approve that plan?
12. **Reflective:** What do we need to do differently next time to make the approval process less bureaucratic?

Tip #2: Use AICA as a deliberate process to plan, organize, and deliver a persuasive message.

A wareness: What do you want the other party to be aware of?

I nterest: Appeal to the other party's interest. Examples of interests include: recognition, security, growth, pride, acceptance, fear, independence, curiosity, status, fulfillment, quality, customer or public service satisfaction, accuracy, image, reputation, teamwork, productivity, and reducing risks.

C ommitment: Don't assume you have the other party's commitment. Ensure that you ask for it.

A ction: Be specific about what action needs to be taken, by whom, by what dates, and by what standards and measurements?

Tip #3: Use the "PARTNER" approach to show empathy by listening to understand without the need to agree or judge.

P rovide honest input with transparency to help make things better for all concerned: Instead of stating, "I don't know how to tell you this, but…." say, "I am concerned that if we try to do this too fast, we might be taking these risks …."

A cknowledge the mutual interests involved: "I agree that there is a more productive way to conduct our collaboration meetings. Let's talk about how we can address our common interest to improve our productivity for this team project. What do you recommend?"

R eframe suggestions and objections based on the collaboration goal: "So I am hearing you say that our current process is not working well to achieve our collaboration goal, right?"

T one should be confident, sincere, and respectful: "I know we made a mistake, and that there were negative impacts. I would like to work with you and get your help to make some changes that will ensure that this does not happen again."

N eutralize using objective, unemotional words: Instead of "you made that mistake," say, "So a mistake was made, and now we need to fix it."

E mpathize, don't criticize. Instead of "I know you meant well, but…" say, "I know you had good intentions, and …."

R esponsibility and accountability are key and it starts with you: Instead of "you should have told me," say "I suggest that next time to avoid this issue, I can … and you can …."

Template 6

Collaboration Conflicts: Strategies for Success

Name:

Date:

Purpose: To analyze a collaboration conflict and plan strategies to address and resolve it successfully.

Instructions:

These questions are designed to help you gain more insights about a specific conflict involved in a collaboration. This includes the context, "triggers", and stage of the conflict. Answer the following questions honestly, and then select the best strategies to use from the list provided for each stage.

Questions to Answer to Gain Insights About the Conflict

1. What is the topic of the conflict generally?
2. Who is involved in the conflict? (Identify titles and roles)
3. Identify possible causes of the conflict.
4. Identify your responses to the conflict:
   - Physiological responses based on flight or fight tendencies, triggering, for example, rapid heart rate, sweating, high adrenaline, nausea, or other digestive issues.

Describe the details:
   - Cognitive responses based on attitudes toward conflict, such as personal and cultural values and beliefs about conflict, and

including: conflict as good or bad, or as something to avoid or fight for at all costs?

Describe the details:

5. What has been done so far to address or attempt to resolve the conflict, and what are the impacts?
6. What is the current stage of the conflict? Choose one of the following answers:

- *Dormant:* The issues of the conflict are not yet visible to those not involved.
- *Emerging:* Tensions between people are becoming more visible to others if they are very observant.
- *Active:* This is the peak of conflict when responses are most obvious and easiest to notice.
- *Aftermath:* The conflict itself is over, and the aftereffects are felt by both those directly involved and observers of the conflict.

Stage Management Strategies for Conflict

Dormant Stage: Invisible

1. Remind those involved that all collaborators need to be able to manage the inevitable tensions and conflicts that occur in collaborations.
2. Create a "safe" team environment where people can voice their concerns openly.
3. Speak confidentially to anyone who asks and provide support and constructive feedback.

Emerging Stage: Small glimpses

1. Ask those parties involved to meet individually to discuss individual and collective concerns and needs.
2. Appoint a facilitator to keep the discussion focused on constructive comments only.

3. Conduct a team meeting to provide further ideas and support for the collaboration issue(s) and concern(s).
4. Remind all parties involved that disagreement in a collaboration can lead to better solutions.
5. Remind all involved about the "ground rules" and group norms for disagreement.

Active Stage: You can't avoid it because it is out in the open

1. Appoint a neutral leader or facilitator to encourage constructive discussion and avoid unnecessary escalations.
2. Get individual and group commitment to follow "ground rules" for addressing the conflict.
3. Adapt an "us against the problem" mindset, instead of a "you are the problem" attitude.
4. Make key points visual to emphasize areas of agreement and disagreement.
5. Ensure sufficient time for less assertive individuals to contribute their views without being dominated by more assertive members.
6. When possible, meet in person to maintain unity and build trust.
7. Avoid overuse of e-mails and social media to maintain trust and confidentiality.
8. Refocus the discussion on the collaboration vision, mission, and goal.
9. Summarize and paraphrase key points of disagreement as well as agreement.
10. Document key agreements and action steps for clarity and to ensure accountability to complete them.
11. Encourage asking questions to understand and explore resolutions, not to judge.
12. Agree on decision-making guidelines and requirements to address conflict-related options and solutions.
13. Do not pressure parties to reach an agreement too soon.
14. Schedule time for reflection to reflect and recover emotionally before making any decisions.

Aftermath Stage: It's over, but the impacts are still felt

1. Capture initial concerns and suggestions in writing, making sure the comments are constructive and not blaming.
2. Conduct post-conflict discussions in person to sustain trust.
3. Remind the group that conflicts are opportunities to learn, grow, innovate, and build trust.
4. Discuss how the conflict was managed: what the group did well, and what needs to change the next time there is disagreement for continuous improvement.

Template 7

Checklist: Generating Creative Ideas on Collaboration Teams

Name:

Date:

Purpose: To become more effective when planning and facilitating idea generation meetings during collaborations to achieve the most creative results.

1. **Cocreate with others and share the credit**
   - Strengthen the group's identity as cocreators by asking them to choose a team name, collaboration vision, team motto, and idea generation goal.
   - Discuss the benefits of group ownership of cocreated ideas.
   - Get legal advice to identify concerns and requirements regarding shared ownership of cocreated ideas, such as intellectual property, use of social media, digital copies of materials, patents, and other relevant legal issues.
   - Agree on guidelines and commitments required from team members for shared ownership of cocreated ideas.
   - Consult a collaboration lawyer to make sure all aspects of shared ownership of ideas are identified and addressed as required.
   - Finalize any necessary changes to contracts, agreements, and other legal documents.
   - Obtain legal advice to ensure that all parties are informed and agree to idea ownership requirements before starting the idea generation sessions.

- Communicate relevant information about shared intellectual property ownership to all collaboration team members.

2. Focus on ideas first, and do not discuss practicalities too soon

- Communicate and enforce clear "ground rules" to stay focused on inventing creative ideas.
- Avoid getting stuck in too many details until all of the ideas have been generated.
- Create a "Parking Lot" list of tactical details to address later after the idea generation stage.
- Schedule a series of dedicated days for idea generation well ahead of time to ensure maximum attendance from team members.
- Make all ideas visual for everyone to see clearly.
- Record the ideas exactly as others say or describe them, without any edits or additions.
- Schedule dedicated meetings for idea generation only, without distractions from other topics.
- Generate a list of stimulating questions to spark creative ideas prior to each idea generation session to give all parties time to prepare ahead of time.
- Set milestones for generating creative ideas and celebrate each milestone.
- Invite creativity experts to join the group to share stories or methods to stimulate better creative idea generation.
- Schedule idea generation meetings during hours when members have maximum energy, to ensure peak productivity.

3. Use all of your brain: left, right, and whole

- Explore using a variety of methods that appeal to different brain types: left, right, and whole.
- Encourage participation by appealing to all three learning styles: visual, auditory, and kinesthetic.

4. Left-brain characteristics

- Prefers a sequential, step-by-step approach.

- Thinks in a compartmentalized way: likes to do things one at a time and allocate time separately for work and home activities.
- Values rules, regulations, guidelines, schedules, and the importance of achieving deadlines.
- Likes checklists, order, routine, consistency, and templates.
- Dislikes inconsistency, missing and inaccurate data, multiple and conflicting priorities, and scheduling time pressures.
- Tends to be a perfectionist, and can be slow to make decisions.

5. **Right-brain characteristics**
- Prefers a nonlinear, inconsistent approach emphasizing free association and sensory input.
- Enjoys imaginative activities: likes to do things spontaneously and have unlimited time to envision ideas.
- Values intuition, spontaneity, imagery, visual clues, big picture, outcomes, and innovative approaches.
- Suspicious of checklists, order, routine, templates, rules, and regulations.
- Can sometimes miss deadlines by preferring to spend time instead on other interests.
- Does not always pay attention to details, resulting in some inaccuracies and inconsistencies.

6. **Whole-brain characteristics**
- Values inconsistency: prefers to change focus frequently between linear and nonlinear, factual and intuitive, and numerical and conceptual ways of thinking.
- Relies on the situation or project context to determine the best approach.
- Balances spontaneity with a scheduled approach to time.
- Distrusts using left- or right-brain methods exclusively.

Template 8

Tips For Overcoming Collaboration Obstacles

Name:

Date:

Purpose: To identify 10 obstacles to effective collaboration and ways to overcome them most effectively.

1. **Obstacle: Unrealistic expectations about collaboration as a process**

   Tips:
   - Identify individual expectations:
     - o Conduct a precollaboration survey.
     - o Conduct precollaboration interviews.
     - o Host a precollaboration meeting to explore expectations for accountability and responsibility from self and others.

   - Agree on group expectations about how to collaborate best with each other:
     - o Facilitate group agreement about what to expect realistically from the collaboration process.
     - o Discuss which expectations are achievable, and which ones are not.
     - o Agree on how to manage the collaboration process best, including roles and responsibilities.
     - o Offer the opportunity to assign a replacement person if participants are not able to agree to commit to the expectations for the collaboration process.

- Identify key checkpoints when the group meets to assess and improve the collaboration process. Invite a collaboration specialist to meet with the group to present information about what to expect from a collaboration process:
  - o Offer advice to the group.
  - o Agree to consult with the group as needed.

- Revise the collaboration goals to make them more achievable for the group:
  - o Make the goals SMART: specific, measurable, achievable, realistic, and time-bound.
  - o Rank the goals as a group, in order of priority.
  - o Agree on the top priorities.

2. **Obstacle: Difficulty scheduling meetings that work for all parties**
   Tips:
   - Assign backup representatives in case one cannot attend.
   - Schedule multiple meetings in clusters to help members plan ahead for maximum attendance by all.
   - Agree on the minimum number of attendees required.
   - Determine scheduling procedures for changes and cancellations and enforce them consistently.
   - Rotate meeting locations.
   - Establish meeting time limits and enforce them.
   - Get agreement on the minimum number of meetings required to maintain one's membership on the collaboration team.

3. **Obstacle: Lack of accountability and commitment to follow through on promises**
   Tips:
   - Require standards for maintaining membership on the collaboration team.
   - Create a team vision that all members are required to be accountable for supporting throughout the collaboration.

- Create a "Collaboration Accountability Team" to help support members with mentoring, information sharing, advice, and access to additional resources that are available.

4. **Obstacle: Incompatible and dominant personalities**
   Tips:
   - Appoint a strong facilitator.
   - Don't take it personally.
   - Communicate the importance of fairness for all to speak and participate equally.
   - Ask the group to identify ways to self-manage dominant behaviors.
   - Assign roles at meetings to encourage dominant personalities to speak less and more quiet personalities to speak more.

5. **Obstacle: Technology tools not integrated for everyone's access and use**
   Tips:
   - Keep it simple by choosing technology that is easy to use.
   - Survey all parties to identify what technologies they use, prefer, and dislike.
   - Assign an IT specialist to be on-call for troubleshooting problems.
   - Test first before implementing.
   - Experiment with technology apps.
   - Ensure that the meeting location has maximum technology access.
   - Avoid the overuse of e-mails.
   - Create a file storage system for accessing and archiving key documents.

6. **Obstacle: Discomfort sharing knowledge and resources**
   Tips:
   - Set expectations from the very beginning about the necessity to share information pertinent to the collaboration.

- Assign subteams with complementary skills and knowledge to work together.
- Select meeting spaces most suitable for information exchange.
- Showcase individual knowledge and talent at group meetings.
- Create an internal knowledge and resource-sharing website for all collaboration partners.

7. **Obstacle: Lack of sponsorship from senior executive leaders**
   Tips:
   - Promote sponsorship to support and streamline decisions.
   - Recruit sponsors at the beginning to endorse the collaboration to support its success.
   - Make the sponsors a part of the team's collaboration success story. Ask them to participate and help promote the collaboration team's ideas and initiatives.

8. **Obstacle: Organizational bureaucracy restricting change initiatives**
   Tips:
   - Determine what processes and policies are involved and required.
   - Identify specific improvements for streamlining policies and procedures that slow down change.
   - Get commitment from bureaucrats involved to help streamline processes:
     o Appeal to their interests.
     o Ask for advice.
     o Conduct a pilot test that they help sponsor and participate in.
     o Use referent power to influence others by gaining more credibility by referring to someone they report to or respect.

9. **Obstacle: Lack of diverse membership and representation**
   Tips:
   - Identify diversity gaps in the group.
   - "Borrow" it: invite more diverse individuals to participate.

- Change it: replace or add additional members intentionally, either full time or for specific meetings when needed.
- Compensate for it: ask for independent feedback from interviews, surveys, or consultants to recommend ways to increase thinking and membership diversity, and allocate a budget for these if required.

10. **Obstacle: Change of leadership and membership within the collaboration team**
    Tips:
    - Review and refine the vision statement.
    - Appoint an orientation team to help newcomers adjust.
    - Appoint someone from within the team to mentor any new leaders and members.

References

Eberle, B. 1996. *Scamper: Games for Imagination Development.* Waco, Texas: Prufrock Press Inc.

Michalko, M. 2006. *Thinkertoys: A Handbook of Creative Thinking Techniques,* 2nd ed. New York, NY: Ten Speed Press.

About the Author

Dr. Gail Levitt is an experienced executive education facilitator, coach, and mentor specializing in influential leadership, negotiating, and collaborating for professionals in both the public and private sectors.

Gail is based in Toronto, Ontario, Canada, and is the President of Levitt Communications Inc. She has two decades of work experience in corporate management and collaborative leadership, plus extensive training and research on collaboration strategies and techniques. This breadth of experience enables Gail to offer both a realistic and refreshing approach that enables her readers and clients to collaborate with optimal success.

Index

OTHER TITLES IN THE HUMAN RESOURCE MANAGEMENT AND ORGANIZATIONAL BEHAVIOR COLLECTION

- *Uniquely Great* by Lucy English
- *The Relevance of Humanities to the 21st Century Workplace* by Michael Edmondson
- *Untenable* by Gary Covert
- *Chief Kickboxing Officer* by Alfonso Asensio
- *No Cape Required* by Bob Hughes and Helen Caton Hughes
- *Cross-Cultural Leadership Studies* by Alan S. Gutterman
- *Comparative Management Studies* by Alan S. Gutterman
- *Women Leaders* by Sapna Welsh
- *Practicing Management* by Alan S. Gutterman
- *Practicing Leadership* by Alan S. Gutterman

Announcing the Business Expert Press Digital Library

Concise e-books business students need for classroom and research

This book can also be purchased in an e-book collection by your library as

- a one-time purchase,
- that is owned forever,
- allows for simultaneous readers,
- has no restrictions on printing, and
- can be downloaded as PDFs from within the library community.

Our digital library collections are a great solution to beat the rising cost of textbooks. E-books can be loaded into their course management systems or onto students' e-book readers.
The **Business Expert Press** digital libraries are very affordable, with no obligation to buy in future years. For more information, please visit **www.businessexpertpress.com/librarians**. To set up a trial in the United States, please email **sales@businessexpertpress.com**.

www.ingramcontent.com/pod-product-compliance
Lightning Source LLC
Chambersburg PA
CBHW061318220326
41599CB00026B/4934